Existential Psychology

Studies in
Psychology

Existential Psychology

Edited by Rollo May

**William Alanson White Institute
of Psychoanalysis, Psychiatry, and Psychology**

Random House
New York

CONTENTS

FOREWORD

Although the existential approach has been most prominent in European psychology and psychiatry for two decades, it was practically unknown in this country until two years ago. Since then, some of us have been concerned that it may become *too* popular in some quarters, particularly in national magazines. But we have been comforted by a saying of Nietzsche's, "The first adherents of a movement are no argument against it."

We have been reassured also on a deeper level by noting that there are, at the moment, two quite different aspects of the interest in existential psychology and psychiatry in this country. The one is the bandwagon trend, always dangerous and particularly unconstructive in the areas of the search for truth and the endeavors to understand man and his relationships. The other kind of interest is the much more quiet, profound, questioning attitude of many of our colleagues who believe that the present dominant images of man in psychology and psychiatry are inadequate and do not give us the foundation we need for our psychotherapy and research.

The papers that follow, with the exception of the bibliography and certain sections added to the first chapter, were presented in the Symposium on Existential Psychology at the Annual Convention of the American Psychological Association in Cincinnati in September, 1959. We accepted the invitation of Random House to publish the papers not only because of the very great interest evidenced in this symposium at its presentation, but also because of our conviction that what is particularly needed in this area is further study. Our hope is that this book may serve as a stimulus to students who are interested in the field and that it may suggest topics and questions to be pursued.

Thus, our purpose is not to give a systematic or definitive account of existential psychology—that cannot be done as yet. And so far as it can be, it has been done in the first three chapters of the volume *Existence* (17)*. These papers are meant rather to show how and why some of us who are interested in existential psychology "got" that way. Some of these papers are impressionistic and are so meant to be. Maslow's chapter is refreshingly direct: What's in existential psychology for us? Feifel's paper illustrates how this approach opens up for psychological inquiry such significant areas as attitudes toward death, heretofore conspicuous by their absence in psychology. My second chapter seeks to present a structural base in existential psychology for psychotherapy. Rogers' paper discusses, in particular, the relation of existential psychology to empirical research, and Allport's comments refer to some of the over-all implications of our inquiries. We trust that Lyons' bibliography will be an aid to students who may wish to read further about the many problems in the field.

ROLLO MAY

* Throughout the text, references in parentheses refer to the bibliography at the end of the volume.

Existential Psychology

CHAPTER I

ROLLO MAY

The Emergence of
Existential Psychology

In this introductory essay, I wish to discuss how existential psychology emerged, particularly on our American scene. I want then to discuss some of the perennial questions that many of us in psychology have been asking, questions that we believe call for an existential approach, and to indicate some of the new slants that this approach gives to certain of our central problems in psychology and psychotherapy. Finally, I want to cite some of the difficulties and the unsolved problems, scientific and otherwise, that confront existential psychology today.

1

It is a curious paradox, we note at the outset, that whereas there is a great deal of hostility and outright anger in this country toward existential psychology, there is at the same time a deep underlying affinity between this approach and our American character and thought in psychology as well as in other areas. The existential approach, for example, is very close to the thought of William James. Take, for example, his emphases on the *immediacy of experience* and *the union of thought and action,* emphases which became passionate in James as they had been in Kierkegaard. Indeed, when Kierkegaard proclaims, "Truth exists for the individual only as he himself produces it in action," the words have a familiar echo to those of us raised in the American pragmatic tradition. Another aspect in William James that expresses the same approach to reality as existential psychology is the importance of *decision and commitment*—his argument that you cannot know truth by sitting in a detached armchair, but that *willing* and *decision* are themselves prerequisites to the discovery of truth. Furthermore, his humaneness and his great breadth as a human being enabled him to bring art and religion into this thought without sacrificing his scientific integrity, another parallel to the existential psychologists.

But this striking parallel is, on closer inspection, not so surprising, for when William James came back from Europe in the latter half of the nineteenth century, he was committed, like Kierkegaard, who had written three decades earlier, to an attack on the reigning panrationalism of Hegel, which identified truth with abstract concepts. Both James and Kierkegaard were dedicated to rediscovering man as a vital, decisive, experiencing being. As Paul Tillich writes,

Like the American philosophers William James and John Dewey, the existential philosophers are appealing from the conclusion of "rationalistic" thinking which equates Reality with the object of thought, with relations or "essences," to Reality as men experience it immediately in their actual living. They consequently take their place with all those who have regarded man's immediate experience as revealing more completely the nature and traits of Reality than man's cognitive experience. (68)

This, of course, indicates, we may remark parenthetically, why those of us interested in psychotherapy are more apt to be concerned with the existential approach than are those of our colleagues involved in laboratory research or the construction of theory, for we have, of necessity, taken our stand with immediate human beings who are suffering, struggling, experiencing conflicts in a multitude of protean forms. This "immediate experiencing" is our milieu, and it gives us the reason as well as the data for our research. We have to be genuinely realistic and "hard-headed" in the respect that we deal with patients whose anxiety and sufferings will not be healed by theories, no matter how brilliant, or by abstract laws, no matter how comprehensive. But by means of this immediate interaction in psychotherapy, we achieve a kind of information and understanding of human beings that we would not get any other way, for no person will disclose the deepest levels of his dreads and hopes, certainly not to another person and usually not even to himself, unless by this painful process of exploring his conflicts he has some hope of overcoming his blockages and alleviating his suffering.

Tillich terms James and Dewey philosophers, but they are, of course, psychologists as well—probably our greatest and most influential, and in many ways our most typically American thinkers. The confluence of these two disciplines indicates another aspect of the existential approach: it deals with psychological categories—"experience," "anxiety," and so forth—but it is concerned with understanding these aspects of man's life on the deeper level which Tillich calls *ontological reality*. It would be an error to think of

existential psychology as a resurrection of the old "philosophical psychology" of the nineteenth century. The
existential approach is not a movement back to the armchair of speculation, but an endeavor to understand man's
behavior and experience in terms of the presuppositions
that underlie them—presuppositions that underlie our
science and our image of man. It is the endeavor to understand the nature of this man who *does* the experiencing
and to *whom* the experiences happen.

Adrian van Kaam, in reviewing the work of the European psychologist J. Linschoten, describes how William
James's search for a new image of man as a broader basis
for psychology led him directly into the center of the development of phenomenology. (Phenomenology, the first
stage in the development of existential psychology, will be
illustrated and defined later.) Van Kaam's summary is so
pertinent to our topic that we quote it in detail.*

> One of the leading European existential phenomenologists,
> J. Linschoten, wrote a book, *Towards a Phenomenology,* with
> the subtitle, "The Psychology of William James." On the fly
> leaf a proposition of William James from his *Talks to
> Teachers* is printed: "A mere bare fraud is just what our
> Western common sense will never believe the phenomenal
> world to be." In the introduction to this book, the diary of
> Husserl is quoted by Linschoten, where the father of Euro-
> pean phenomenology admits the influence of the thought of
> this great American, James, on his own thinking.
>
> The book demonstrates in a well documented way that the
> hidden intention of James' thinking has been realized in the
> breakthrough of the new existential cultural awareness.
> James was groping towards a vaguely felt new phase in the
> history of Western mankind. Rooted in the former cultural
> period, he favored psychology as it was practiced, but he
> expressed continuous dissatisfaction with this exclusively

* Adrian van Kaam, "The impact of existential phenomenology on the psychological literature of western Europe," paper
to be published in *Review of Existential Psychology and Psychiatry,* 1 (1), 1961, pp. 62-91.

onesided way of "existing" * in the world. Linschoten concludes, in his final chapter, that James was on the road towards a phenomenological psychology before Buytendijk, Merleau-Ponty, and Straus, and was already ahead of them in his concern for the *integration of an objectifying psychology within the frame of a descriptive psychology*.

The genius of James foresaw the anthropological phase [the problem of the concept of man] of the new cultural period before his contemporaries were even aware of the first two phases. James contended that a mechanistic interpretation of the world could be integrated with a teleological interpretation. This is because they are views of various modes of existing in the same "experienced" world. One should realize that "the deeper features of reality are found only in perceptual experience," that various modes of standing out in the world *must* lead *necessarily* to seeing the phenomena in different constellations, *must* lead to different questions from which different answers *must* result.

The lack of systematization in James' work is based on the insight that the unity of man and of the world are not dependent on "the one rational method" but on the unity of the prerational world, the one world of experience, the one original integral source of the diverging questions which make for different sciences and different psychologies. This original integral source of all ways of existing in the world is the body, the origin of experience of the world. This origin of experience has two aspects: that which is the source of the experience and that which is experienced itself. Therefore, one can choose one of two viewpoints: one can describe and analyze experience and body as the original modes of standing out within the world as has been done by such men as Merleau-Ponty, Strauss, and Buytendijk; or one can describe and analyze experience and body in the time-space coherence of the experienced "reality" as has been done by such men as Skinner, Hull, Spence. The first

* [Van Kaam uses "existing" here and elsewhere in its strict etymological sense of "standing out" toward something (*ex-sistere*), meaning a way of relating to the world. Various psychologies, for example, are different ways of relating to the world.—Editor.]

way leads to what has been called a *descriptive* psychology, the second one to an *explaining* psychology. As soon as one of them makes its viewpoint absolute, they are no longer able to communicate with one another. James has tried to preserve their complementary mutuality. This is possible only on the basis of a theory of man as an integral source of experience, a theory of his original mode of existing, a phenomenology of the experienced world, which phenomenology is implicit in James.*

2

At this point we pause to define our terms. Existentialism means centering upon the *existing* person; it is the emphasis on the human being as he is *emerging, becoming*. The word "existence" comes from the root *ex-sistere*, meaning literally "to stand out, emerge." Traditionally in Western culture, *existence* has been set over against *essence*, the latter being the emphasis upon immutable principles, truth, logical laws, etc., that are supposed to stand above any given existence. In endeavoring to separate reality into its discrete parts and to formulate abstract laws for these parts, Western science has by and large been *essentialist* in character; mathematics is the ultimate, pure form of this essentialist approach. In psychology, the endeavors to see human beings in terms of forces, drives, conditioned reflexes, and so on, illustrate the approach via essences.

The emphasis on essences was dominant in Western thought and science—with such notable exceptions, to name only a few, as Socrates, Augustine, and Pascal—until roughly a hundred years ago. The "peak" was reached, the most systematic and comprehensive expression of "essentialism," in Hegel's panrationalism, an endeavor to encompass all reality in a system of concepts that identified reality with abstract thought. It was against Hegel that

* J. Linschoten, *Op weg naar een fenomenologische psychologie.* Utrecht: Bijleveld, 1959 and *Die Psychologie von William James.* Berlin: De Gruyter, 1961.

Kierkegaard, and later Nietzsche, revolted so strenuously. (The reader who wishes to follow this historical development in greater detail is referred to the first chapter of *Existence* [17].)

But in the decades since World War I, the existential approach has emerged from the status of stepchild of Western culture to a dominant position in the center of Western art, literature, theology, and philosophy. It has gone hand in hand with the new developments in science, particularly the physics of Bohr and Heisenberg.

The extreme of the existentialist position is found in Jean Paul Sartre's statement that "existence precedes essence," the assertion that only as we affirm our existence do we have any essence at all. This is a consistent part of Sartre's great emphasis on decision: "We *are* our choices."

My own position, and that of most psychologists who appreciate the great value of this existential revolution, is not so extreme as Sartre's. "Essences" must not be ruled out—they are presupposed in logic, mathematical forms, and other aspects of truth which are not dependent upon any individual's decision or whim. But that is not to say that you can adequately describe or understand a living human being, or any living organism, on an "essentialist" basis. *There is no such thing as truth or reality for a living human being except as he participates in it, is conscious of it, has some relationship to it.* We can demonstrate at every moment of the day in our psychotherapeutic work that only the truth that comes alive, becomes more than an abstract idea, and is "felt on the pulse," only the truth that is genuinely experienced on all levels of being, including what is called subconscious and unconscious and never excluding the element of conscious decision and responsibility—only this truth has the power to change a human being.

The existentialist emphasis in psychology does not, therefore, deny the validity of the approaches based on conditioning, the formulation of drives, the study of discrete mechanisms, and so on. It only holds that you can never explain or understand any *living* human being on that basis. And the harm arises when the image of man, the presuppositions about man himself are exclusively based on such methods. There seems to be the following "law" at work: <u>the more accurately and comprehensively you can describe a given mechanism, the more you lose</u> the existing person. *The more absolutely and completely you formulate the forces or drives, the more you are talking about abstractions and not the existing, living human being.* For the living person (who is not hypnotized or drugged or in some other way placed in an artificial position, such as in a laboratory, in which his element of decision and his responsibility for his own existence are temporarily suspended for the purposes of the experiment) always transcends the given mechanism and always experiences the "drive" or "force" in his unique way. The distinction is whether the "person has meaning in terms of the mechanism" or the "mechanism has meaning in terms of the person." The existential emphasis is firmly on the latter. And it holds that the former can be integrated within the latter.

True, the term "existentialist" is dubious and confused these days, associated as it is with the beatnik movement at one extreme and with esoteric, untranslatable, Germanic, philosophical concepts at the other. True also, the movement collects the "lunatic fringe" groups—to which existential psychology and psychiatry are by no means immune. I often ask myself whether in some quarters the term has become so dubious as to be no longer useful. But "existence" does have the important historical meanings outlined above and probably, therefore, can and ought to be saved from its deteriorated forms.

In psychology and psychiatry, the term demarcates an *attitude,* an approach to human beings, rather than a special school or group. It is doubtful whether it makes sense to speak of "*an* existential psychologist or psychotherapist" in contradistinction to other schools; it is not a system of therapy but an attitude toward therapy, not a set of new techniques but a concern with the understanding of the structure of the human being and his experience that must underlie all techniques. This is why it makes sense, if I may say so without being misunderstood, to say that every psychotherapist is existential to the extent that he is a good therapist, i.e., that he is able to grasp the patient in his reality and is characterized by the kinds of understanding and presence that will be discussed below.

3

I wish, after these sallies at definition, to *be* existentialist in this essay and to speak directly from my own experience as a person and as a practicing psychoanalytic psychotherapist. Some fifteen years ago, when I was working on my book, *The Meaning of Anxiety*, I spent a year and a half in bed in a tuberculosis sanatorium. I had a great deal of time to ponder the meaning of anxiety—and plenty of first hand data in myself and my fellow patients. In the course of this time, I studied the only two books written on anxiety till our day, *The Problem of Anxiety* by Freud and *The Concept of Dread* by Kierkegaard. I valued Freud's formulations: namely, his first theory, that anxiety is the re-emergence of repressed libido, and his second, that anxiety is the ego's reaction to the threat of the loss of the loved object. Kierkegaard, on the other hand, described anxiety as the struggle of the living being against non-being—which I could immediately experience there in my struggle with death or the prospect of being a life-long invalid. He went on to point out that the real terror in anxiety is not this death as such, but the fact that each of us within himself is on both sides of the fight, that "anxiety is a desire for what one dreads," as he put it; thus, like an "alien power it lays hold of an individual, and yet one cannot tear one's self away."

What struck me powerfully then, was that Kierkegaard was writing about *exactly what my fellow patients and I were going through.* Freud was not; he was writing on a different level, giving formulations of the psychic mechanisms by which anxiety comes about. Kierkegaard was portraying what is immediately experienced by human beings in crisis. It was, specifically, the crisis of life against death, which was completely real to us patients, but he was writing about a crisis that I believe is not in its essential form different from the various crises of people who come for therapy, or the crises that all of us experience in much more minute form a dozen times a day, even though we push the ultimate prospect of death far from our minds. Freud was writing on the technical level, where his genius was supreme; perhaps more than any man up to his time, he *knew about anxiety.* Kierkegaard, a genius of a different order, was writing on the existential, ontological level; he *knew anxiety.*

This is not a value dichotomy; obviously both are necessary. Our real problem, rather, is given us by our cultural-historical situation. We in the Western world are the heirs of four centuries of technical achievement in power over nature and now over ourselves; this is our greatness and, at the same time it is also our greatest peril. We are not in danger of repressing the technical emphasis (of which Freud's tremendous popularity in this country is proof if any were necessary). But rather we repress the opposite. If I may use terms which I shall be discussing and defining more fully later, we repress the *sense of being,* the *ontological sense.* One consequence of this repression of the sense of being is that modern man's image of himself, his experience and concept of himself as a responsible individual have likewise disintegrated.

I make no apologies in admitting that I take very seriously, as will have been evident already, the dehumanizing dangers in our tendency in modern science to make man over into the image of the machine, into the image of the techniques by which we study him. This tendency is not the fault of any "dangerous" men or "vicious" schools; it is rather a crisis brought upon us by our particular historical predicament. Karl Jaspers, both psychiatrist and existentialist philosopher, holds that we are actually in process of losing self-consciousness and that we may well be in the last age of historical man. William Whyte, in his *Organization Man*, cautions that modern man's enemies may turn out to be a "mild-looking group of therapists, who . . . would be doing what they did to help you." He refers here to the tendency to use the social sciences in support of the social ethic of our historical period; and thus the process of helping people may actually make them conform and tend toward the destruction of individuality. We cannot brush aside the cautions of such men as unintelligent or antiscientific; to try to do so would make *us* the obscurantists. There is a real possibility that we may be helping the individual adjust and be happy at the price of loss of his being.

One may agree with my sentiments here but hold that the existentialist approach, with these terms "being" and "nonbeing," may not be of much help. Some readers will already have concluded that their suspicion was only too right, that this so-called existential approach in psychology is hopelessly vague and horribly muddled. Carl Rogers remarks in a later chapter that many American psychologists must find these terms abhorrent because they sound so general, so philosophical, so untestable. Rogers goes on to point out, however, that he had no difficulty in putting the existential principles in therapy into empirically testable hypotheses.

But I would go further and hold that *without* some concepts of "being" and "non-being" we cannot even understand our most commonly used psychological mechanisms. Take for example, *repression, resistance,* and *transference*. The usual discussions of these terms hang in midair, it seems to me, unconvincing and psychologically unreal, precisely because we have lacked an underlying structure on which to base them. The term "repression,"

for example, obviously refers to a phenomenon we observe
all the time, a dynamism which Freud clearly, and in many
forms, described. The mechanism is generally explained
by saying that the child represses into unconsciousness
certain impulses, such as sex and hostility, because the culture, in the form of parental figures, disapproves, and the
child must protect his own security with these figures. But
this culture which assumedly disapproves is made up of the
very same people who do the repressing. Is it not an illusion, therefore, and much too simple, to speak of the culture over against the individual in such fashion and to
make it our whipping boy? Furthermore, where did we get
the idea that children or adults are so concerned with
security and libidinal satisfactions? Are these not carry-
overs from our work with the *neurotic, anxious* child and
the *neurotic* adult?

Certainly the neurotic, anxious child *is* compulsively
concerned with security, for example; and certainly the
neurotic adult, and we who study him, read our later
formulations back into the unsuspecting mind of the child.
But is not the normal child just as truly interested in
moving out into the world, exploring, following his
curiosity and sense of adventure—going out "to learn to
shivver and to shake," as the nursery rhyme puts it? And
if you block these needs of the child, do you not get a
traumatic reaction from him just as you do when you take
away his security? I, for one, believe we vastly over-
emphasize the human being's concern with security and
survival satisfactions because they so neatly fit our cause-
and-effect way of thinking. I believe Nietzsche and Kierkegaard were more accurate when they described man as
*the organism who makes certain values—prestige, power,
tenderness, love—more important than pleasure and even
more important than survival itself.**

---

* This is the point Binswanger is making in the case of *Ellen
West,* translated in the volume *Existence* (17). By means of the
discussion of the psychological illness and suicide of Ellen

The implication of our argument here is that we can understand such a mechanism as repression, for example, only on the deeper level of the meaning of the human beings' potentialities. In this respect, "being" is to be defined as the *individual's unique pattern of potentialities*. These potentialities will be partly shared with other individuals but will in every case form a unique pattern for this particular person.

We must ask these questions, therefore, if we are to understand repression in a given person: What is this person's relation to his own potentialities? What goes on that he chooses, or is forced to choose, to block off from his awareness something that he knows, and on another level

West, he asks whether there are times when an existence, in order to fulfill itself, must destroy its existence. In this case, Binswanger, like so many of his European psychiatric and psychological colleagues, discusses a case for the purpose of delving into the understanding of some problem about human beings rather than for the purpose of illustrating how the case should or should not be managed therapeutically. In presenting the case, we assumed, as editors of *Existence*, that it, like the other cases, would be understood on the basis of the purposes and assumptions of its author in writing it; this was an unrealistic assumption. The case is almost universally discussed—and from that point of view justly criticized—in this country from the point of view of what therapy should have been given Ellen West. If it had been Binswanger's purpose to discuss techniques of therapy, he would not have taken a case from the archives of four and a half decades ago in his sanatorium. He seeks, rather, to ask this most profound of all questions: Does the human being have needs and values that transcend its own survival, and are there not situations when the existence, in order to fulfill itself, needs to destroy itself? The implication of this question is in the most radical way to question simple adaptation, length of life, and survival as ultimate goals. It is similar to Nietzsche's point referred to above, and also similar to Maslow's emphasis when he brings out that the "self-actualizing personalities" that he studied resist acculturation.

knows that he knows? In my own work in psychotherapy, there appears more and more evidence that anxiety in our day arises not so much out of fear of lack of libidinal satisfactions or security, but rather out of the patient's fear of his own powers and the conflicts that arise from that fear. This may well be the particular "neurotic personality of our time"—the neurotic pattern of contemporary "outer-directed," organizational man.

The "unconscious," then, is not to be thought of as a reservoir of impulses, thoughts, and wishes that are culturally unacceptable. I define it rather as *those potentialities for knowing and experiencing that the individual cannot or will not actualize.* On this level, we shall find that the simple mechanism of repression, which we blithely started with, is infinitely less simple than it looks; that it involves a complex struggle of the individual's *being* against the possibility of *non-being;* that it cannot be adequately comprehended in "ego" and "not-ego" terms, or even "self" and "not-self"; and that it inescapably raises the question of the human being's freedom with respect to his own potentialities. This margin of freedom must be assumed if one is to deal with an existing person. In this margin resides the individual's responsibility for himself, which even the therapist cannot take away.

Thus, every mechanism or dynanism, every force or drive, presupposes an underlying structure that is infinitely greater than the mechanism, drive, or force itself. And note that I do not say it is the "sum total" of the mechanisms, et cetera. It is not the "sum total," though it includes all the mechanisms, drives, or forces: it is the underlying structure from which they derive their meaning. This structure is, to use one definition proposed above, the *pattern of potentiality* of the living individual man *of whom* the mechanism is one expression; the given mechanism is one of a multitude of ways in which he actualizes his potentiality. Surely, you can abstract a given mechanism like "repression" or "regression" for study and arrive at formulations of forces and drives which seem to be operative; but your study will have meaning only if you say at every point, "I am abstracting such and such a form of behavior," and if you also make clear at every point *what* you are abstracting *from,* namely the living man who *has* these experiences, the man *to whom* these things happen.

4

In a similar vein, I have, for a number of years, been struck, as a practicing therapist and teacher of therapists, by how often our concern with trying to understand the patient in terms of the mechanisms by which his behavior takes place blocks our understanding of what he really is experiencing. Here is a patient, Mrs. Hutchens (about whom I shall center some of my remarks in Chapter IV), who comes into my office for the first time, a suburban woman in her middle thirties, who tries to keep her expression poised and sophisticated. But no one could fail to see in her eyes something of the terror of a frightened animal or a lost child. I know, from what her neurological specialists have already told me, that her presenting problem is hysterical tenseness of the larynx, as a result of which she can talk only with a perpetual hoarseness. I have been given the hypothesis from her Rorschach that she has felt all her life, "If I say what I really feel, I'll be rejected; under these conditions it is better not to talk at all." During this first hour with her, I also get some hints of the genetic *why* of her problem as she tells me of her authoritarian relation with her mother and grandmother and of *how* she learned to guard firmly against telling any secrets at all.

But if, as I sit here, I am chiefly thinking of these *whys* and *hows* of the way the problem came about, I will have grasped everything *except the most important thing of all, the existing person.* Indeed, I will have grasped everything except the only real source of data I have, namely, this experiencing human being, this person now emerging, becoming, "building world," as the existential psychologists put it, immediately in this room with me.

This is where *phenomenology,* the first stage in the existential psychotherapeutic movement, has been a helpful breakthrough for many of us. Phenomenology is the endeavor to take the phenomena as given. It is the disciplined effort to clear one's mind of the presuppositions that so often cause us to see in the patient only our own theories or the dogmas of our own systems, the effort to experience instead the phenomena in their full reality as they present themselves. It is the attitude of openness and readiness to hear—aspects of the art of listening in psychotherapy that are generally taken for granted and sound so easy but are exceedingly difficult.

Note that we say *experience* the phenomena and not *observe;* for we need to be able, as far as possible, to catch what the patient is communicating on many different levels; these include not only the words he utters but his facial expressions, his gestures, the distance from us at which he sits, various feelings which he will have and communicate subtly to the therapist and will serve as messages even though he cannot verbalize them directly, ad infinitum. And there is always a great deal of subliminal communication on levels below what either the patient or therapist may be conscious of at the moment. This points toward a controversial area in therapy which is most difficult in the training and practice of therapists, but which is unavoidable because it is so important, namely, subliminal, empathetic, "telepathic" communication. We shall not go into it here; I wish only to say this experiencing of the communications of the patient on many different levels at once is one aspect of what the existential psychiatrists like Binswanger call *presence.*

Phenomenology requires an "attitude of disciplined naïveté," in Robert MacLeod's phrase. And commenting on this phrase, Albert Wellek adds his own, "an ability to *experience critically*" (97). It is not possible, in my judgment, to listen to any words or even to give one's attention to anything without some assumed concepts, some constructs in one's own mind by which he hears, by which he orients himself in his world at that moment. But the important terms "disciplined" in MacLeod's phrase and "critically" in Wellek's refer, I take it, to the difficult attainment of objectivity—that while one must have constructs as he listens, one's aim in therapy is to make one's own constructs sufficiently flexible so that he can listen in terms of the patient's constructs and hear in the patient's language.

Phenomenology has many complex ramifications, particularly as developed by Edmund Husserl, who decisively influenced not only the philosophers Heidegger and Sartre but also the psychiatrists Minkowski, Straus, and Binswanger, the psychologists Buytendijk, Merleau-Ponty, and many others. We shall not go into these ramifications here. (The student may find a survey of psychological phenomenology in Ellenberger's chapter in *Existence* and may pursue it further in the references in the bibliography at the end of this book.)

Sometimes the phenomenological emphasis in psychotherapy is used as a disparagement of the learning of technique or as a reason for not studying the problems of diagnosis and clinical dynamics. I think this is an error. What is important, rather, is to apprehend the fact that the technical and diagnostic concerns are on a different level from the understanding that takes place in the immediate encounter in therapy. The mistake is in confusing them or letting one absorb the other. The student and practicing psychologist must steer his course between the Scylla of letting knowledge of techniques be a substitute for direct understanding and communication with the patient and the Charybdis of assuming that he acts in a rarified atmosphere of clinical purity without any constructs at all.

Certainly it is true that students learning therapy often

become preoccupied with techniques; this is the strongest anxiety-allaying mechanism available to them in the turmoil-fraught encounters in psychotherapy. Indeed, one of the strongest motivations for dogmatism and rigid formulations among psychotherapeutic and analytic schools of all sorts lies right here—the technical dogma protects the psychologist and psychiatrist from their own anxiety. But to that extent, the techniques also protect the psychologist or psychiatrist from understanding the patient; they block him off from the full presence in the encounter which is essential to understanding what is going on. One student in a case seminar on existential psychotherapy put it succinctly when he remarked that the chief thing he had learned was that "understanding does not follow knowledge of dynamics."

There is, however, a danger of "wild eclecticism" in these phenomenological and existential approaches to therapy when they are used without the rigorous clinical study and thought which precedes any expertness. Knowledge of techniques and the rigorous study of dynamics in the training of the psychotherapist should be presupposed. Our situation is analogous to the artist: long and expert training is necessary, but if, at the moment of painting, the artist is preoccupied with technique or technical questions —a preoccupation every artist knows arises exactly at those points at which some anxiety overtakes him—he can be sure nothing creative will go on. Diagnosis is a legitimate and necessary function, particularly at the beginning of therapy; but it is a function different from the therapy itself and requires a different attitude and orientation to the patient. There is something to be said for the attitude that once one gets into therapy with a patient and has decided on the general direction, one forgets for the time being the diagnostic question. By the same token, questions of technique will arise in the therapist's mind from time to time as the therapy proceeds, and one of the characteristics of existential psychotherapy is that the technique changes. These changes will not be hit and miss, however, but will depend on the needs of the patient at given times.

If this discussion sounds unconcluded and gives the appearance of straddling the issue of "technique" on one side and "understanding" on the other, the appearance is indeed correct. The whole topic of the "technical-objective" versus the "understanding-subjective" attitude has been on a false dichotomized basis in our psychological and psychiatric discussions. It needs to be restated on the basis of the concept of the existence of the patient as *being-in-the-world,* and the therapist as existing in and participating in this world. I shall not essay such a restatement here, but I wish only to state my conviction that such a reformulation is possible and gives promise of taking us out of our present dichotomy on this topic. And in the meantime, I wish as a practical expedient to take my stand against the nascent anti-rational tendencies in the existential approach. Though I believe that therapists are born and not made, it inheres in one's integrity to be cognizant of the fact that there also is a great deal we can learn!

5

Another question that has perennially perplexed many of us in psychology has already been implied above, and we now turn to it explicitly. What are the presuppositions which underlie our science and our practice? I do not say "scientific method" here; already a good deal of attention has been paid, and rightly, to the problem of methodology. But every method is based on certain presuppositions— assumptions about the nature of man, the nature of his experience, and so forth. These presuppositions are partially conditioned by our culture and by the particular point in history at which we stand. As far as I can see, this crucial area is almost always covered over in psychology: we tend to assume uncritically and implicitly that our particular method is true for all time. The statement that science has built-in self-corrective measures—which is partially true—cannot be taken as a reason for overlooking the fact that our particular science is culturally and historically conditioned and is thereby limited even in its self-corrective measures.

At this point, the existential insistence is that, because every psychology, every way of understanding man, is based upon certain presuppositions, the psychologist must continually analyze and clarify his own presuppositions. One's presuppositions always limit and constrict what one sees in a problem, experiment, or therapeutic situation; from this aspect of our human "finiteness" there is no escape. The naturalist perceives in man what fits his naturalistic spectacles; the positivist sees the aspects of experience that fit the logical forms of his propositions; and it is well known that different therapists of different schools will see in the same dream of a single patient the dynamics that fit the theory of their particular school. The old parable of the blind men and the elephant is writ large on the activities of men in the enlightened twentieth century as well as those of earlier, more "benighted" ages. Bertrand Russell puts the problem well with respect to physical science: "Physics is mathematical not because we know so much about the physical world but because we know so little; it is only its mathematical properties that we can discover."

No one, physicist, psychologist, or anyone else, can leap out of his historically conditioned skin. But the one way we can keep the presuppositions underlying our particular method from undue biasing effect is to know consciously what they are and so not to absolutize or dogmatize them. Thus we have at least a chance of refraining from forcing our subjects or patients upon our "procrustean couches" and lopping off, or refusing to see, what does not fit.

In Ludwig Binswanger's little book relating his conversations and correspondence with Freud, *Sigmund Freud:*

Reminiscences of a Friendship (84), there are some interesting interchanges illustrating this point. The friendship between Freud, the psychoanalyst, and Binswanger, a leading existential psychiatrist of Switzerland, was lifelong and tender, and it marks the only instance of Freud's continuing in friendship with someone who differed radically with him.

Shortly before Freud's eightieth birthday, Binswanger wrote an essay describing how Freud's theory had radically deepened clinical psychiatry, but he added that Freud's own existence as a person pointed beyond the deterministic presuppositions of his theory. "Now [with Freud's psychoanalytic contribution] man is no longer merely an animated organism, but a 'living being' who has origins in the finite life process of this earth, and who dies its life and lives its death; illness is no longer an externally or internally caused disturbance of the 'normal' course of a life on the way to its death." But Binswanger went on to point out that as a result of his interest in existential analysis, he believed that in Freud's theory man is not yet man in the full sense of the word:

> . . . for to be a man does not mean merely to be a creature begotten by living-dying life, cast into it and beaten about, and put in high spirits or low spirits by it; it means to be a being that looks its own and mankind's fate in the face, a being that is "steadfast," i.e., one taking its own stance, or one standing on its own feet. . . . The fact that our lives are determined by the forces of life, is only one side of the truth; the other is that we determine these forces as our fate. Only the two sides together can take in the full problem of sanity and insanity. Those who, like Freud, have forged their fates with the hammer—the work of art he has created in the medium of language is sufficient evidence of this—can dispute this fact least of all (*ibid.*).

Then, on the occasion of Freud's eightieth birthday, the Viennese Medical Society invited Binswanger, along with

Thomas Mann, to deliver papers at the anniversary celebration. Freud himself did not attend, not being in good
health and also, as he wrote Binswanger, not being fond
of anniversary celebrations. ("They seem to be on the
American model.") Binswanger spent two days with
Freud in Vienna at the time of this birthday and remarked
that in these conversations he was again impressed by
how far Freud's own largeness and depth of humanity as
a man surpassed his scientific theories.

In his paper at the celebration, Binswanger gave credit
to Freud for having enlarged and deepened our insight
into human nature more, perhaps, than anyone since Aristotle. But he went on to point out that these insights wore
"a theoretic-scientific garb that as a whole appeared to me
too 'one-sided' and narrow." He held that Freud's great
contribution was in the area of *homo natura,* man in relation to nature (*Umwelt*)—drives, instincts, and similar
aspects of experience. And as a consequence, Binswanger
believed that in Freud's theory there was only a shadowy,
epiphenomenal understanding of man in relation to his
fellowmen (*Mitwelt*) and that the area of man in relation
to himself (*Eigenwelt*) was omitted entirely.

Binswanger sent a copy of the paper to Freud and a week
later received a letter from him containing the following
sentences:

As I read it I was delighted with your beautiful language,
your erudition, the vastness of your horizon, your tactfulness
in contradicting me. As is well known, one can put up with
vast quantities of praise. . . . *Naturally, for all that you have
failed to convince me.** I have always confined myself to
the ground floor and basement of the edifice. You maintain
that by changing one's point of view, one can also see the
upper story, in which dwell such distinguished guests as
religion, art, etc. . . . I have already found a place for
religion, by putting it under the category of "the neurosis
of mankind." But probably we are speaking at cross purposes,

* Binswanger's italics.

and our differences will be ironed out only after centuries. In cordial friendship, and with greetings to your charming wife, your Freud (*ibid.*, p. 99).

Binswanger then adds in his book—and this is the central reason we quote the interchange—"As can be seen from the last sentence, Freud looked upon our differences as something to be surmounted by empirical investigation, not as something bearing upon the transcendental* conceptions that underly all empirical research."

In my judgment, Binswanger's point is irrefutable. One can gather empirical data, let us say on religion and art, from now till doomsday, and one will never get any closer to understanding these activities if, to start with, his presuppositions shut out what the religious person is dedicated to and what the artist is trying to do. Deterministic presuppositions make it possible to understand everything about art except the creative act and the art itself; mechanistic naturalistic presuppositions may undercover many facts about religion, but, as in Freud's terms, religion will always turn out to be more or less a neurosis, and what the genuinely religious person is concerned with will never get into the picture at all.

The point we wish to make in this discussion is the necessity of analyzing the presuppositions one assumes and of making allowance for the sectors of reality—which may be large indeed—that one's particular approach necessarily leaves out. In my judgment, we in psychology have often truncated our understanding and distorted our perception by failure consciously to clarify these presuppositions.

I vividly recall how, back in my graduate days in psychology some twenty years ago, Freud's theories tended to be dismissed as "unscientific" because they did not fit the

---

* By "transcendental," Binswanger of course does not refer to anything ethereal or magical: he means the underlying presuppositions which "point beyond" the given fact, the presuppositions which determine the goals of one's activity.

methods then in vogue in graduate schools of psychology. I maintained at the time that this missed the point: Freud had uncovered realms of human experience of tremendous importance, and if they did not fit our methods, so much the worse for our methods; the problem was to devise new ones. In actual fact, the methods did catch up—perhaps, one should add, with a vengeance, until, as Rogers has stated, Freudianism is now the dogma of American clinical psychology. Remembering my own graduate-school days, I am therefore inclined to smile when someone says that the concepts of existential psychology are "unscientific" because they do not fit the particular methods *now* in vogue.

It is certainly clear that the Freudian mechanisms invite the separation into discrete cause-and-effect formulations which fit the deterministic methodology dominant in American psychology. But what also needs to be seen is that this making of Freudianism into the dogma of psychology has been accomplished at the price of omitting essential and vitally important aspects of Freud's thought. There is at present a three-cornered liaison, in tendency and to some extent in actuality, between Freudianism, behaviorism in psychology, and positivism in philosophy. An example of the first side of the liaison is the great similarity between Hull's drive-reduction theory of learning and Freud's concept of pleasure, the goal of behavior, as consisting of the reduction of stimuli. An example of the second is the statement of the philosopher Herman Feigl in his address at a recent annual convention of the American Psychological Association, that Freud's specific mechanisms could be formulated and used scientifically, but such concepts as the "death instinct" could not be.

But the trouble there is that such concepts as the "death instinct" in Freud were precisely what saved him from the full mechanistic implications of his system; these concepts always point beyond the deterministic limitations of his theory. They are, in the best sense of the word, a mythology. Freud was never content to let go of this mythological dimension to his thinking despite his great effort at the same time to formulate psychology in terms of his nineteenth-century biological presuppositions. In my judgment, his mythology is fundamental to the greatness of his contribution and essential to his central discoveries, such as "the unconscious." It was likewise essential to his radical contribution to the new image of man, namely, man as pushed by demonic, tragic, and destructive forces. I have tried elsewhere to show that Freud's tragic concept of the Oedipus is much closer to the truth than our tendency to interpret the Oedipus complex in terms of discrete sexual and hostile relationships in the family. The formulation of the "death instinct" as a biological instinct makes no sense, of course, and in this sense is rightly rejected by American behaviorism and positivism. But as a psychological and spiritual statement of the tragic nature of man, the idea has very great importance indeed and transcends any purely biological or mechanistic interpretation.

Methodology always suffers from a cultural lag. Our problem is to open our vision to more of human experience, to develop and free our methods so that they will as far as possible do justice to the richness and breadth of man's experience. This can be done only by analysing the philosophical presuppositions. As Maslow pithily states in Chapter II, "It is extremely important for psychologists that the existentialists may supply psychology with the underlying philosophy which it now lacks. At any rate, the basic philosophical problems will surely be opened up for discussion again, and perhaps psychologists will stop relying on pseudosolutions or on unconscious unexamined philosophies they picked up as children."

6

Having made the above point, we must hasten to add that this does not solve all the difficult questions of the relation of the existential approach to science. There is, of course, the legitimate question of how such propositions as those in existential psychology and psychotherapy can be tested. In Chapter V, Carl Rogers indicates, in a beginning way, how "ontological principles" can be studied and tested in empirical psychology. At Harvard, "tests derived from existential categories have already been formulated," Lawrence Pervin writes (57). In New York, there are several seminars in existential psychotherapy which endeavor to clarify this approach. These steps lie ahead; but I do not see any insuperable problems in the direction of studying existential propositions scientifically, provided that we are not limited to particular methods, say of natural science.

A more perplexing and tricky question arises with respect to the problem of prediction in science. How much and to what extent does one insist that science be able to predict the behavior of the given individual? Pervin cites as one of the inadequacies of the existential approach the fact that in as much as it conceives of the individual as free and unique, it makes his behavior unlawful and unpredictable. But "predictable" is a highly ambiguous term. And "lawful" and "predictable" cannot be identified. What we find in psychotherapy is that the behavior of the *neurotic* personality can be predicted fairly rigidly; this is because his behavior is the product of compulsive patterns and drives. But although the healthy person is "predictable" in the sense that his behavior is integrated and he can be depended upon to act according to his own character, he always at the same time shows a *new* element in his behavior. His actions are fresh, spontaneous, interesting, and in this sense he is just the opposite of the neurotic and his predictability. This is the essence of creativity. Maslow again puts this well: "Only the flexibly creative person can really manage future, only the one who can face novelty with confidence and without fear. I am convinced that much of what we now call psychology is the study of the tricks we use to avoid the anxiety of absolute novelty by making believe the future will be like the past."

I do not wish to offer solutions to these issues here, which indeed I could not do anyway. I only wish to indicate that we need to open up our view of science. Allport's idiographic psychology is a highly important step; Rogers' work is another example of a significant trend in the developing of science not limited to the old presuppositions. This concern for a new breadth is not at all limited to those in the so-called existential wing of psychology. In the symposium "Clinical Skills Revisited," which just preceded the one at which the papers in this book were initially read, Richard Dana discussed the situation of training graduate students in psychology.

> I suspect that the common, salient outcome of our previous four or five (or six) graduate years was caution—not breadth or depth of scholarship or ability to generalize— but mere caution. A kind of trained adherence to limited inferences from data collected under rigorous conditions of control. Caution is indeed necessary in diagnostic testing or treating of other persons but caution alone is stifling and blinding for either individuals or professions. . . . We possess the methodological sophistication; we lack the grand concepts and may be diminishing our professional potential for generation of theory by exclusive preoccupation with science. To be sure, we must be scientists but we also must be *sapient* humans, first.

The existential psychological position is, in my judgment, not at all antiscientific. But it does insist that it would be ironic indeed if our very dedication to certain methodologies in psychology should itself blind us in our understanding of human beings. Helen Sargent was expressing the mood of many of us when she remarked, "Science offers more leeway than graduate students are permitted to realize."

Adrian van Kaam very pertinently demonstrates how the

phenomenological and existential approach is significant even for experimental psychology in his discussion of the work of Linschoten of Utrecht and J. Ex, an experimental psychologist at the University of Nijmegen:

> J. Linschoten, director of the psychological laboratory of the university of Utrecht, has clarified the relationship between existential phenomenology and experimental psychology. He has made clear that precise and adequate experimental research requires a phenomenological investigation of the essential characteristics of the phenomenon under study, and he defined the phenomenological description as a necessary prerequisite for a greater exactness in experimentation. He proved that the phenomenological analysis which shows the essential characteristics and the essential structure of the phenomenon which has to be experimented on has necessarily a temporal and logical priority to the experiment itself. Further, the use of the phenomenological method in order to obtain a greater exactness in the experimentation does not mean a change in the experimental techniques itself. The necessity of phenomenological analysis of the situation is based by Linschoten on the fact that there is no phenomenon or act or experiment which is not bound to a situation. Secondly there is no situation which does not imply an explicit or implicit presence of the human person. Finally it is never possible to bypass the influence of the human person in a situation. He also makes us aware of the fact that results which are discovered in a situation A can never be declared as valid for a situation B as long as one has not proved by a phenomenological analysis the structural identity of situation A and B.*
>
> J. Ex wrote a book concerning analysis of the situation and social-psychological experiment. He mentions the drawbacks of neglecting phenomenal analysis of the situation and illustrates this by proving extensively how Sherif's interpretation of his quantitative data obtained in his classical experiment of 1935 was mistaken because of his neglect of a phenomenal analysis of the situation. He also shows how a phenomenal analysis of the situation leads to the devising of a new experiment which can correct the mistakes of Sherif.

* J. Linschoten, *Das Experiment in der phaenomenologischen Psychologie*. Unpublished paper, Bonn, 1955.

At the end of his work he gives the data of some other experiments based on an analysis of the situation.

The method of existential phenomenology used in this way leads to a re-examination of the classical experiments and a correction of possible inexactness due to the absence of these existential criteria. It would lead us too far astray to mention the various experiments which are re-examined and corrected in this way and the new experiments which are set up with these new, more strict pre-experimental controls now available (176).*

7

Let me propose here several principles which I believe need to be included as guiding lines in a science to serve as a basis for psychotherapy. First, the science must be relevant to the distinguishing characteristics of what we are trying to understand, in this case the human being. It must be relevant, that is, to the distinctive qualities and characteristics that constitute the human being as *human,* that constitute the self as self, characteristics without which this being would not be what he is, namely, a human being.

A second guiding principle is in opposition to the assumption in conventional science that we explain the more complex by the more simple. This is generally taken on the model of evolution: the organisms and activities higher on the evolutionary scale are explained by those lower. But this is only half the truth. It is just as true that when a new level of complexity emerges (such as self-consciousness in man), this level becomes decisive for our understanding of all previous levels. In this sense, the *simpler can be understood and explained only in terms of the more complex*. This point is particularly important for psychology and is discussed more fully with the topic of self-consciousness (p. 78).

A third guiding principle is this: Our fundamental unit

* J. Ex, Situatie-analyse on sociaalpsychologisch experiment. Bussum, Holland: Paul Brand, 1957.

of study in psychotherapy is not a "problem" that the patient brings in, such as impotence; or a pattern, such as a neurotic pattern of sado-masochism or a diagnostic category of sickness, such as hysteria or phobia, ad infinitum; or a drive or pattern of drives. Our unit of study is, rather, *two-persons-existing-in-a-world, the world at the moment being represented by the consulting room of the therapist.* To be sure, the patient brings in all his problems, his "illness," his past history, and everything else simply because it is an integral part of him; but what is important to see clearly is that the one datum that has reality at the time is that he creates a certain world in the consulting room, and it is in the context of this world that some understanding of his being-in-his-world may emerge. This world and the understanding of it is something in which both persons, patient and therapist, participate. Our point here has far-reaching implications not only because it bears directly on our research and practice in psychotherapy, but also because it suggests the guiding lines of an existential approach to science.

8

There are several areas in which the existential approach adds new dimensions to our usual psychological studies that I should like to cite not only as illustrations of what this approach is trying to do, but also as topics in which students may be interested in further study and research.

The first is the existential emphasis on *will and decision.* One of Freud's great contributions lay in his cutting through the futility and self-deceit in Victorian "will power" as the faculty by which our forefathers "made resolutions" and purportedly directed their lives in the way the culture said they should go. Freud uncovered the vast areas in which behavior and motives are determined by "unconscious" urges, drives, fears, past experiences, and so forth. He was entirely accurate in this diagnosis of the morbid side of Victorian "will power."

But along with this emphasis there went an unavoidable undermining of the functions of will and decision themselves and a likewise unavoidable emphasis upon man as determined, driven, "lived *by* the unconscious," as Freud, agreeing with the words of Groddeck, put it. This had the effect of playing into modern man's pervasive tendency— which has become almost a disease in the middle of the twentieth century—to see himself as passive, the willy-nilly product of the powerful juggernaut of economic forces (as Marx demonstrated with a brilliant analysis on the socioeconomic level parallel to Freud's). And of late years this tendency has spread to include contemporary man's conviction that he is the helpless victim of scientific forces in the atom bomb, about the use of which the citizen in the street feels powerless to do anything. A central core of modern man's "neurosis" is the undermining of his experience of himself as responsible, the sapping of his willing and decision. And this lack of will is much more than merely an ethical problem: modern man so often has the conviction that even if he *did* exert his "will" and capacity for decision, they would not make any difference anyway.

It was against precisely these trends that the existentialists like Kierkegaard and Nietzsche made their strongest, most vehement stand. And it is in the light of modern man's broken will that the existential emphases of Schopenhauer, with his world as "will and idea," Bergson, with his *"élan vital,"* William James, with his "will to believe," are to be understood.

The protest of the existentialists was violent and at times desperate (as in Nietzsche), at other times noble, especially courageous (as in the resistance movement of Camus and Sartre), even if it seemed to many observers to be ineffectual against the on-moving lava of conformism, collectivism, and the robot man. The existentialists' central proclamation is this: No matter how great the forces victimizing the human being, man has the capacity to *know* that he is being victimized, and thus to influence in some way how he will relate *to* his fate. There is never lost that kernel of the power to take some stand, to make some decision, no matter how minute. This is why they hold that man's existence consists, in the last analysis, of his freedom. Heidegger even goes on (in a fascinating essay) to define truth as freedom. Tillich phrased it beautifully in a recent speech, "Man becomes truly human only at the moment of decision."

The implications of this position for psychology and psychotherapy are, of course, profound. In general, in our academic psychological tradition, we have tended to accept the position, no matter what individual psychologists themselves believed about their own ethical actions, that as psychologists we were concerned only with what is determined and could be understood in a deterministic framework. This limitation of perception, of course, tended inevitably to make our man into the image of what we let ourselves see.

In psychoanalysis and psychotherapy the problem became more critical and could not long be avoided, for the theory and process of psychoanalysis and most other forms of psychotherapy inevitably played into the passive tendencies of the patient. As Otto Rank and Wilhelm Reich in the 1920's began to point out, there were built-in tendencies in psychoanalysis that themselves sapped its vitality and tended to emasculate not only the reality with which psychoanalysis deals, but the power and inclination of the patient to change. In the early days of psychoanalysis, when revelations of the unconscious had an obvious "shock value," this problem did not come out so much into the open; and in any case with hysterical patients, who formed the bulk of those Freud worked with in his early formative years, there does exist a special dynamic in what Freud could call "repressed libido" pushing for expression. But now that most of our patients are "compulsives" of one form or another, and everybody knows about the Oedipus complex, and our patients talk about sex with an apparent freedom which would have shocked Freud's Victorian patients off the couch (and, indeed, talking about sex is perhaps the easiest way of avoiding really making any *decisions* about love and sexual relatedness), the problem of the undermining of will and decision cannot longer be avoided. The "repetition compulsion," a problem that has always remained intractable and insoluble within the context of classical psychoanalysis, is in my judgment fundamentally related to this dilemma about will and decisions.

Other forms of psychotherapy do not escape the dilemma of psychoanalysis; namely, the process of psychotherapy itself has built-in tendencies which invite the patient to relinquish his position as the deciding agent. The very name "patient" proposes it! Not only do the automatic supportive elements in therapy have this tendency, but likewise the tendency to search for everything else as responsible for one's problems rather than one's self.* To be sure psychotherapists of all stripes and schools realize that sooner or later the patient must make some decisions, learn to take some responsibility for himself; but the theory and the technique of most psychotherapy tends to be built on exactly the opposite premise.

The existential approach in psychology and psychotherapy holds that we cannot leave will and decision to chance, on the assumption that ultimately the patient "somehow happens" to make a decision, or slides into a decision by ennui, default, or mutual fatigue with the therapist, or from sensing that the therapist (now the benevolent parent) will approve of him if he does take such and such steps. The existential approach puts decision and will back into the center of the picture. Not at all in the sense of "free will against determinism"; this issue

* I am not, of course, arguing against causality, genetic or otherwise. I am arguing against a passive, "patient" attitude toward these "causes" of one's fate.

is dead and buried. Nor in the sense of denying what Freud describes as unconscious experience; these deterministic factors certainly operate, and the existentialists, who make much of "finiteness" and man's limitations, certainly know this. They hold, however, that *in the revealing and exploring of these deterministic forces in the patient's life, the patient is orienting himself in some particular way to the data and thus is engaged in some choice, no matter how seemingly insignificant; is experiencing some freedom, no matter how subtle*. The existential attitude in psychotherapy does not at all "push" the patient into decisions; indeed, I am convinced that it is only by this clarification of the patient's powers of will and decision that the therapist can *avoid* inadvertently and subtly pushing the patient in one direction or another. The point is that self-consciousness itself—the person's awareness that the vast, complex, protean flow of experience is *his* experience—brings in inseparably the element of decision at the moment.

We are, of course, using the terms "will" and "decision" in a way that does not at all refer exclusively to the momentous and life-shaping decisions only; the words have infinitely more extensive and subtle meaning. And though perception always involves decision (the act, for example, of electing what you are going to attend to), we do not at all identify the two. Decision always involves some element that is not only not determined by the outside situation but not even *given* in the external situation; it involves some element of leap, some taking of a chance, some movement of one's self in a direction which one can never fully predict before the leap. The mature human being (i.e., one who is not rigidly constricted and determined by neurotic compulsive patterns) is then ready to make the new orientation, the new "decision," in this new spot in which he finds himself. The "new place" I refer to may be as simple and non-world-shaking as any new idea I find myself entertaining or any new memory that pops up in a seemingly random chain of free association.

Thus, I believe the process of decisiveness we are discussing is present in every act of consciousness.

The interested student will find a good deal of material at hand with which to study this problem, despite the fact that to date very little exists in specifically psychological literature. The possibilities for study and research would seem to be endless and fascinating.

Another topic on which the existential approach breaks new ground is the *problem of the ego*. I say "problem" advisedly: the ego has come into the center of psychoanalytic and psychological discussions lately, and although the interest in it reflects a highly positive development, I believe the term itself causes more problems than it solves. It is especially important to discuss it here, albeit briefly, because many psychologists assume that what existential psychology is talking about is encompassed in psychoanalytic ego psychology. This is an error.

Freud originally described the ego as weak and passive, a monarch not in command in his own house, pushed by the id on one side and the superego on the other. Later he gave to the ego the executive functions and specifically described it as being the organizing center of the personality.* But he still saw the ego as essentially weak. I think he was right on that point, for by virtue of its structural position in the ego-id-superego system, the ego must remain fundamentally without autonomy even in its own realm, as we shall point out below.

In the last few years, in response to contemporary man's great need for autonomy and a sense of identity, considerable interest has swung to "ego psychology" in the psychoanalytic movement. But what has resulted has been the handing over to the ego of the functions of autonomy, sense of identity, synthesis of experience, and other functions, more or less arbitrarily arrived at, which we suddenly discover the human being has to have. The result in the orthodox analytic movement is that many "egos"

* *The ego and the id* (London, 1927).

appear. Karl Menninger* speaks of the "observing ego," the "regressive ego," the "reality ego," the "healthy ego," et cetera. A Freudian colleague and friend of mine congratulated me after a speech in which I had attacked this concept of a horde of egos by remarking, with obvious irony, that I had a good "synthetic ego"! Some psychoanalysts now speak of "multiple egos in the same personality," referring not to neurotic personalities but to the so-called normal ones. To my mind "multiple egos" is a precise description of a *neurotic* personality.

The concept of the ego, with its capacity for being broken up into many discrete "egos," is tempting for experimental psychology, for it invites the "divide and conquer" method of study that we have inherited in our traditional dichotomized scientific method. But I am convinced that it has grave inadequacies, practically and theoretically. It is as though we suddenly voted our weak monarch many new powers; but the monarch becomes all the more frightened and nonplused because the throne on which he sits is in its very framework weak and unsound and his new powers only overwhelm him and confuse him the more.

For in this picture of many different egos, where has the principle of organization vanished to? If you have this multitude of egos, you have by definition lost the center of organization, the center of unity that any executive must have if he is to function as an executive. If it is countered that this picture of the multitude of egos reflects the fragmentation of contemporary man, I would rejoin that any concept of fragmentation presupposes some unity *of which* it is a fragmentation. Rapaport writes an essay entitled "The Autonomy of the Ego" as part of the recent development we are referring to; Jung has a chapter in one of his books entitled "The Autonomy of the Unconscious"; and someone could write an essay, following Cannon's

* *The theory of psychoanalytic therapy* (New York, 1958).

"Wisdom of the Body," entitled "The Autonomy of the Body." Each would have a partial truth; but would not each be fundamentally wrong? For neither the "ego" nor the "unconscious" nor the body can be autonomous. Autonomy by its very nature can be located only in the *centered self*.

To be sure, the work of Erickson and Wheelis on identity—which I value highly—goes beyond the presuppositions of the orthodox system in psychoanalysis with respect to the ego and, therefore, it seems to me, is able to offer something of significance in this area. In my judgment, the value of their work lies precisely at those points at which it does break the bounds of the previous system; and the ultimate limitations of their approach, as in the final chapters of Wheelis' *Quest for Identity,* seem to me to inhere in the impossibility of constructing a new basis within the traditional psychoanalytic framework.

I could conclude this point more comfortably if I had a nice solution to propose. But I do not. I can blame this situation partly on the limitations of our English language: the terms we must use, like "self" and "being," are woefully inadequate.

But whatever terms we use, we must ask ourselves certain questions when we are dealing with the question of the ego. Particularly we must ask these questions when we consider the proposals at hand about the many different "egos" and their functions, such as "regression" and "reality testing." We need to ask: At what point do I experience the fact that *I am the one who has these different egos?* What unity do I presuppose *of which* the various egos are fragments? Such questions indicate that logically as well as psychologically, we must go behind the ego-id-superego system and endeavor to understand the "being" of whom these are different expressions. My self, or my being (the two at this point are parallel), is to be found at that center at which I know myself as the one responding in these different ways, the center at which I experience myself as the one behaving in the ways described by these varied functions.

The tentative hypothesis I suggest is that my "being"—which by definition must have unity if it is to survive as a being*—has three aspects, which we may term "self," "person," and "ego." The "self" I use as the subjective center, the experiencing of the fact that I am the one who behaves in thus and thus ways; the "person" we may take as the aspect in which I am accepted by others, the "persona" of Jung, the social roles of William James; and the "ego" we may take as Freud originally enunciated it, the specific organ of perception by which the self sees and relates to the outside world. I hold no ultimate brief for this hypothesis at the moment; it calls for further clarification, and I offer it here for its suggestive possibilities. But the point I do wish to make strongly is that *being* must be presupposed in discussions of ego and identity, and that the *centered self** must be basic to such discussions.

Other topics that the existential approach in psychology presents in a fresh light, topics that would be fruitful for study in addition to those of *will and decision* and the *problem of the ego* are: the constructive functions of anxiety and guilt; the concept and experience of *being-in-the-world*—a concept which, though it has parallels to gestalt psychology on the formal side, operates on a different level and has exceedingly wide implications; *the significance of time,* particularly future time, as indicated by Maslow in Chapter II.

9

Some of the difficulties and dangers in the existential approach in psychology have already been mentioned, but here we need, finally, to state several of them more explicitly. One difficulty lies in the fact that the concepts in existential psychology lend themselves to being used in the

---

* These points are discussed more fully in Chapter IV.

service of *intellectualistic detachment*. Such terms as "onto-logical" and "ontic" illustrate this; even the term "existen-tial" may of course be used to cover up a multitude of ways of relating (or not relating) to reality which would seem to be most unexistential. The special seductiveness of the terms in this field is that they give a *semblance* of deal-ing with human reality when they may not be doing so at all. Obviously, we need first of all to confront our real experience, in psychotherapy and other forms of psychol-ogy, and then find the terms (which may not be the terms inherited from our European colleagues) which will most fully express and communicate this experience.

Another difficulty or danger in this approach is, para-doxically, just the opposite, namely, the use of the existen-tial approach in the service of anti-intellectualism. It would be an ironic pity indeed if this approach were to be allied, covertly or overtly, with the anti-intellectual tendencies that are now present in the country; certainly this was one of the abuses to which the existential movement in Europe fell unhappy heir. I do not refer here centrally to the beatnik movement in this country; anti-rational, to be sure, the beatnik movement is an endeavor to achieve a con-viction of the subjective reality of the given moment of sense experience, and in this respect the movement has its understandable function, truncated and inadequate as it may be.

But the tendency to distrust reason as such in our culture has arisen from the fact that the alternatives pre-sented to intelligent and sensitive people have seemed to be only arid rationalism on the one hand, in which one saves one's mind by losing one's soul, or vitalis-tic romanticism on the other, in which there has seemed at least a chance of saving one's soul for the time being. The existential approach is certainly opposed to the first; but to make a more difficult and subtle point, I am con-vinced it is opposed to the second as well. The existential approach in psychology as elsewhere is *not to be ration-*

*alistic or antirationalistic, but to seek the ground on which
both reason and unreason are based.* This is what was
sought by Kierkegaard, who was marvelously gifted
logically and intellectually but preferred to be called a
poet; this ground underlying both reason and unreason was
what Nietzsche sought also and what he tried to reveal in
his allegories and shafts of dazzling insight. We must not
be "mis-ologists," Socrates cautioned us. But the "logos,"
the word that expresses and reveals reason, must be made
flesh.

Another difficulty and danger in the existential approach
lies, in my judgment, in its identification in some quarters
with Zen Buddhism. What I am to say here is not a criticism of Zen Buddhism as such; I respect it highly as a
religious-philosophical attitude toward life, and I see its
radical value for modern Western man as a corrective to
the extreme historical emphases to which our Western
culture is heir in its one-sided way, as all cultural developments are one-sided. The psychology of the East is a
corrective for the West and vice versa. But if Zen Buddhism
is to be taken on as a way of life itself by any Western
individual, decades of religious discipline for him are
obviously required. The danger in the identification of
existential psychology with Zen Buddhism is the oversim-
plification of both. It becomes a way of avoiding the difficult problems of anxiety and guilt to which we as Western
men are heir. Indeed, whenever an attitude toward life,
whether it be psychological, philosophical, aesthetic,
or religious, is taken over from another culture, its adherents are invited to jump out of their own cultural
skins; problems are oversimplified and by-passed because
they are not present in the new attitude one takes over.
Kierkegaard and, so far as I know, all the thinkers in the
existential tradition down to Paul Tillich, insist that the
problems of anxiety, guilt, ennui, and conflict of Western
man cannot be avoided. Central in the existential tradition
is the "either/or" emphasis, namely, only with a heightened

awareness of these problems and decisions about them can they be met. In my judgment, the existential approach is the achieving of individuality (including subjective individuality) not by by-passing or avoiding the conflictual realities of the world in which we immediately find ourselves— for us, the Western world—but by confronting these conflicts directly and, *through* the meeting of them, achieving one's individuality.

May I say in conclusion to this discursive but, I hope, helpful chapter that it should be clear that we have not tried to propose a new system or a set of dogma. And the reader will note in the succeeding papers that not one of the contributors does this. Each says, in effect: "The existential development is, to my mind, important and significant; how does it cast light upon our present problems in psychology?" As the reader will have discovered for himself, my own attitude is one of doubt toward the tendencies to make existential psychology a new movement, but it is an attitude of strong affirmation of the penetrating questions about our presuppositions and our image of man asked by this approach. I strongly affirm also the insistence of the existential attitude that these questions be answered on the *human* level. I believe that there is in this approach the demand for and the guiding principles toward a psychology that will be relevant to man's distinguishing characteristics as man. It points, as Gordon Allport says in Chapter VI, toward a psychology of mankind.

CHAPTER II

A. H. MASLOW

Existential Psychology—
What's In It For Us?

I am not an existentialist, nor am I even a careful and thorough student of this movement. There is much in the existentialist writings that I find extremely difficult, or even impossible, to understand and that I have not made much effort to struggle with.

I must confess also that I have studied existentialism not so much for its own sake as in the spirit of, "What's in it for me as a psychologist?" trying all the time to translate it into terms I could use. Perhaps this is why I have found it to be not so much a totally new revelation as a stressing, confirming, sharpening, and rediscovering of trends already existing in American psychology (the various self psychologies, growth psychologies, self-actualization psychologies, organismic psychologies, certain neo-Freudian psychologies, the Jungian psychology, not to mention some of the psychoanalytic ego psychologists, the Gestalt therapists, and I don't know how many more).

For this and other reasons, reading the existentialists has been for me a very interesting, gratifying, and instructive experience. And I think this will also be true for many other psychologists, especially those who are interested in personality theory and in clinical psychology. It has enriched, enlarged, corrected, and strengthened my thinking about the human personality, even though it has not necessitated any fundamental reconstruction.

First of all, permit me to define existentialism in a personal way, in terms of "what's in it for me." To me it means essentially a radical stress on the concept of identity and the experience of identity as a *sine qua non* of human nature and of any philosophy or science of human nature. I choose this concept as *the* basic one partly because I understand it better than terms like essence, existence, and ontology and partly because I also feel that it can be worked with empirically, if not now, then soon.

But then a paradox results, for the Americans have *also* been impressed with the quest for identity (Allport, Rogers, Goldstein, Fromm, Wheelis, Erikson, Horney, May, *et al.*). And I must say that these writers are a lot clearer and a lot closer to raw fact, that is, more empirical than are, e.g., the Germans Heidegger and Jaspers.

(1) Conclusion number one is, then, that the Europeans and Americans are not so far apart as appears at first. We Americans have been "talking prose all the time and didn't know it." Partly, of course, this simultaneous development in different countries is itself an indication that the people who have independently been coming to the same conclusions are all responding to something real outside themselves.

(2) This something real is, I believe, the total collapse of all sources of values outside the individual. Many European existentialists are largely reacting to Nietzsche's conclu-

sion that God is dead and perhaps to the fact that Marx also is dead. The Americans have learned that political democracy and economic prosperity do not in themselves solve any of the basic value problems. There is no place else to turn but inward, to the self, as the locus of values. Paradoxically, even some of the religious existentialists will go along with this conclusion part of the way.

(3) It is extremely important for psychologists that the existentialists may supply psychology with the underlying philosophy that it now lacks. Logical positivism has been a failure, especially for clinical and personality psychologists. At any rate, the basic philosophical problems will surely be opened up for discussion again, and perhaps psychologists will stop relying on pseudosolutions or on unconscious, unexamined philosophies that they picked up as children.

(4) An alternative phrasing of the core (for us Americans) of European existentialism is that it deals radically with that human predicament presented by the gap between human aspirations and human limitations (between what the human being *is,* what he would *like* to be, and what he *could* be). This is not so far off from the identity problem as it might at first sound. A person is both actuality *and* potentiality.

That serious concern with this discrepancy could revolutionize psychology, there is no doubt in my mind. Various literatures already support such a conclusion, e.g., projective testing, self-actualization, the various peak experiences (in which this gap is bridged), the Jungian psychologies, various theological thinkers.

Not only this, but they raise also the problems and techniques of integration of this twofold nature of man, his lower and his higher, his creatureliness and his Godlikeness. On the whole, most philosophies and religions, Eastern as well as Western, have dichotomized them, teaching that the way to become "higher" is to renounce and master "the lower." The existentialists however, teach that *both* are simultaneously defining characteristics of human nature. Neither can be repudiated; they can only be integrated. But we already know something of these integration techniques—of insight, of intellect in the broader sense, of love, of creativeness, of humor and tragedy, of play, of art. I suspect we will focus our studies on these integrative techniques more than we have in the past. Another consequence for my thinking of this stress on the twofold nature of man is the realization that some problems must remain eternally insoluble.

(5) From this flows naturally a concern with the ideal, authentic, or perfect, or Godlike human being, a study of human potentialities as *now* existing in a certain sense, as *current* knowable reality. This, too, may sound merely literary, but it is not. I remind you that this is just a fancy way of asking the old, unanswered questions, "What are the goals of therapy, of education, of bringing up children?"

It also implies another truth and another problem that calls urgently for attention. Practically every serious description of the "authentic person" extant implies that such a person, by virtue of what he has become, assumes a new relation to his society and, indeed, to society in general. He not only transcends himself in various ways; he also transcends his culture. He resists enculturation. He becomes more detached from his culture and from his society. He becomes a little more a member of his species and a little less a member of his local group. My feeling is that most sociologists and anthropologists will take this hard. I therefore confidently expect controversy in this area.

(6) From the European writers, we can and should pick up their greater emphasis on what they call "philosophical anthropology," that is, the attempt to define man, and the differences between man and any other species, between man and objects, and between man and

robots. What are his unique and defining characteristics? What is as essential to man that without it he would no longer be defined as a man?

On the whole, this is a task from which American psychology has abdicated. The various behaviorisms do not generate any such definition, at least none that can be taken seriously. (What *would* an S-R man be like?) Freud's picture of man was clearly unsuitable, leaving out as it did his aspirations, his realizable hopes, his Godlike qualities. The fact that he supplied us with our most comprehensive systems of psychopathology and psychotherapy is beside the point, as the contemporary ego psychologists are finding out.

(7) The Europeans are stressing the self-making of the self, in a way that the Americans do not. Both the Freudians and the self-actualization and growth theorists in this country talk more about discovering the *self* (as if it were there waiting to be found) and of *uncovering* therapy (shovel away the top layers and you will see what has been always lying there, hidden). To say, however, that the self is a project and is *altogether* created by the continual choices of the person himself is almost surely an overstatement in view of what we know of, e.g., the constitutional and genetic determinants of personality. This clash of opinion is a problem that can be settled empirically.

(8) A problem we psychologists have been ducking is the problem of responsibility and, necessarily tied in with it, the concepts of courage and of will in the personality. Perhaps this is close to what the psychoanalysts are now calling "ego strength."

(9) American psychologists have listened to Allport's call for an idiographic psychology but have not done much about it. Not even the clinical psychologists have. We now have an added push from the phenomenologists and existentialists in this direction, one that will be *very* hard to

resist, indeed, I think, theoretically *impossible* to resist. If the study of the uniqueness of the individual does not fit into what we know of science, then so much the worse for the conception of science. It, too, will have to endure 1e-creation.

(10) Phenomenology has a history in American psychological thinking, but on the whole I think it has languished. The European phenomenologists, with their excruciatingly careful and laborious demonstrations, can reteach us that the best way of understanding another human being, or at least *a* way necessary for some purposes, is to get into *his* *Weltanschauung* and to be able to see *his* world through *his* eyes. Of course such a conclusion is rough on any positivistic philosophy of science.

(11) The existentialist stress on the ultimate aloneness of the individual is a useful reminder for us not only to work out further the concepts of decision, of responsibility, of choice, of self-creation, of autonomy, of identity itself. It also makes more problematic and more fascinating the mystery of communication between alonenesses via, e.g., intuition and empathy, love and altruism, identification with others, and homonomy in general. We take these for granted. It would be better if we regarded them as miracles to be explained.

(12) Another preoccupation of existentialist writers can be phrased very simply, I think. It is the dimension of seriousness and profundity of living (or perhaps the "tragic sense of life") contrasted with the shallow and superficial life, which is a kind of diminished living, a defense against the ultimate problems of life. This is not just a literary concept. It has real operational meaning, for instance, in psychotherapy. I (and others) have been increasingly impressed with the fact that tragedy can sometimes be therapeutic and that therapy often seems to work best when people are *driven* into it by pain. It is when the shallow life does not work that it is questioned and that there

occurs a call to fundamentals. Shallowness in psychology does not work either, as the existentialists are demonstrating very clearly.

(13) The existentialists, along with many other groups, are helping to teach us about the limits of verbal, analytic, conceptual rationality. They are part of the current call back to raw experience as prior to any concepts or abstractions. This amounts to what I believe to be a justified critique of the whole way of thinking of the Western world in the twentieth century, including orthodox positivistic science and philosophy, both of which badly need re-examination.

(14) Possibly most important of all the changes to be wrought by phenomenologists and existentialists is an overdue revolution in the theory of science. I should not say "wrought by," but rather "helped along by," because there are many other forces helping to destroy the official philosophy of science or "scientism." It is not only the Cartesian split between subject and object that needs to be overcome. There are other radical changes made necessary by the inclusion of the psyche and of raw experience in reality, and such a change will affect not only the science of psychology but all other sciences as well. For example, parsimony, simplicity, precision, orderliness, logic, elegance, definition are all of the realm of abstraction.

(15) I close with the stimulus that has most powerfully affected me in the existentialist literature, namely, the problem of future time in psychology. Not that this, like all the other problems or pushes I have mentioned up to this point, was totally unfamiliar to me, nor, I imagine, to *any* serious student of the theory of personality. The writings of Charlotte Buhler, of Gordon Allport, and of Kurt Goldstein should also have sensitized us to the necessity of grappling with and systematizing the dynamic role of the future in the presently existing personality, e.g., growth and becoming and possibility necessarily point toward the future, as do the concepts of potentiality and

hoping and of wishing and imagining; reduction to the concrete is a loss of future; threat and apprehension point to the future (no future = no neurosis); self-actualization is meaningless without reference to a currently active future; life can be a gestalt in time, etc., etc.

And yet the *basic and central* importance of this problem for the existentialists has something to teach us, e.g., Erwin Strauss's paper in *Existence* (17). I think it fair to say that no theory of psychology will ever be complete that does not centrally incorporate the concept that man has his future within him, dynamically active at this present moment. In this sense, the future can be treated as ahistorical in Kurt Lewin's sense. Also we must realize that *only* the future is *in principle* unknown and unknowable, which means that all habits, defenses, and coping mechanisms are doubtful and ambiguous because they are based on past experience. Only the flexibly creative person can really manage future, *only* the one who can face novelty with confidence and without fear. I am convinced that much of what we now call psychology is the study of the tricks we use to avoid the anxiety of absolute novelty by making believe the future will be like the past.

I have tried to say that every European stress has its American equivalent. I do not think that this has been clear enough. I have recommended to Rollo May a companion American volume to the one he has already turned out. And of course most of all this represents my hope that we are witnessing an expansion of psychology, not a new "ism" that could turn into an antipsychology or into an antiscience.

It is possible that existentialism will not only enrich psychology. It may also be an additional push toward the establishment of another *branch* of psychology, the psychology of the fully evolved and authentic self and its ways of being. Sutich has suggested calling this onto-psychology.

Certainly it seems more and more clear that what we call "normal" in psychology is really a psychopathology of the average, so undramatic and so widely spread that we do not even notice it ordinarily. The existentialist's study of the authentic person and of authentic living helps to throw this general phoniness, this living by illusions and by fear, into a harsh, clear light which reveals it clearly as sickness, even though widely shared.

I do not think we need take too seriously the European existentialists' harping on dread, on anguish, on despair, and the like, for which their only remedy seems to be to keep a stiff upper lip. This high-I.Q. whimpering on a cosmic scale occurs whenever an external source of values fails to work. They should have learned from the psychotherapists that the loss of illusions and the discovery of identity, though painful at first, can be ultimately exhilarating and strengthening.

CHAPTER III

HERMAN FEIFEL

Death—Relevant Variable
in Psychology *

Even after looking hard into the imposing literature, both important and unimportant, which psychology encompasses, one is impressed by how slim and neglected is the systematized knowledge about attitudes toward death. This is surprising on a number of counts:

(1) Throughout man's history, the idea of death poses the eternal mystery which is the core of some of our most important religious and philosophical systems of thoughts, e.g., Christianity, wherein the meaning of life is consum-

* A portion of this paper is based upon work supported by a research grant, M-2920, from the National Institute of Mental Health, Public Health Service, and some of the material has already appeared in *The Meaning of Death,* ed. H. Feifel (New York: McGraw-Hill, 1959).

mated in its termination; existentialism and its striking pre-occupation with dread and death. This outlook has enormous practical consequences in all spheres of life, economic and political, as well as moral and religious.

(2) One of the more distinguishing characteristics of man, in contrast to other species, is his capacity to grasp the concept of a future—and inevitable death. In chemistry and physics, a "fact" is almost always determined by events that have preceded it; in human beings, present behavior is dependent not only on the past but even more potently, perhaps, by orientation toward future events. Indeed, what a person seeks to become may well, at times, decide to what he attends in his past. The past is an image that changes with our image of ourselves.

(3) Death is something that happens to each one of us. Even before its actual arrival, it is an absent presence. Some hold that fear of death is a universal reaction and that no one is free from it.* When we stop to consider the matter, the notion of the uniqueness and individuality of each one of us gathers full meaning only in realizing that we must die. And it is in this same encounter with death that each of us discovers his hunger for immortality.

(4) A little closer to the psychological hearth, Freud postulated the presence of an unconscious death wish in people, which he connected with certain tendencies toward self-destruction. Melanie Klein believes fear of death to be at the root of all persecutory ideas and so indirectly of all anxiety. Paul Tillich (33), the theologian, whose influence has made itself felt in American psychiatry, bases his theory of anxiety on the ontological statement that man is finite, subject to non-being. Insecurity may well be a symbol of death. Any loss may represent total loss. Jung sees the second half of life as being dominated by the individual's

* F. S. Caprio, "A study of some psychological reactions during prepubescence to the idea of death," *Psychiat. Quart.*, 1950, 24, 495-505; G. Zilboorg, "Fear of death," *Psychoanal. Quart.*, 1943, 12, 465-475.

attitudes toward death. In sum, there is growing recognition of the relationship between mental illness and one's philosophy of life and death.

Death themes and fantasies are prominent in psychopathology. Ideas about death are recurrent in some neurotic patients* and in the hallucinations of many psychotic individuals. There is the stupor of the catatonic patient, sometimes likened to a death state, and the delusions of immortality in certain schizophrenics. It has occurred to me that schizophrenic denial of reality may function, in certain cases, as a magical holding back, if not undoing, of the possibility of death. If living leads inevitably to death, then death can be fended off by not living. Also, a number of psychoanalysts† are of the opinion that one of the main reasons that shock measures produce positive effects in patients is that these treatments provide them with a kind of death-and-rebirth fantasy experience. It is relevant to note, nevertheless, that even when anxiety about death is discussed in the psychiatric literature, it is often interpreted essentially as a derivative or secondary phenomenon, frequently as a more easily endurable aspect of "castration fear" or as separation anxiety from or loss of the love object.‡

* W. Bromberg and P. Schilder, "The attitudes of psychoneurotics toward death," *Psychoanal. Rev.*, 1936, 23, 1-28; J. D. Teicher, " 'Combat fatigue' or death anxiety neurosis," *J. Nerv. Ment. Dis.*, 1953, 117, 234-243; A. Boisen, R. L. Jenkins, and M. Lorr, "Schizophrenic ideation as a striving toward the solution of conflict," *J. Clin. Psychol.*, 1954, 10, 388-391.

† E. g., O. Fenichel, *The psychoanalytic theory of neuroses* (New York: Norton, 1945); P. Schilder, "Notes on the psychology of metrazol treatment of schizophrenia," *J. Nerv. Ment. Dis.*, 1939, 89, 133-144; I. Silbermann, "The psychical experiences during the shocks in shock therapy," *Int. J. Psychoanal.*, 1940, 21, 179-200.

‡ C. W. Wahl, "The fear of death," *Bull. Menninger Clin.*, 1958, 22, 214-223.

(5) Further investigation of attitudes toward death can enrich and deepen our grasp of adaptive and maladaptive reactions to stress and of personality theory in general. The adaptation of the older person to the idea of death, for example, may well be a crucial aspect of the aging process; and study of attitudes toward death in the seriously ill and dying person, an experiment-in-nature, can provide us with fresh insights into the ways different individuals cope with severe threat.

In broader perspective, not only psychology but Western culture generally, in the presence of death, has tended to run, hide, and seek refuge in euphemistic language, in the development of an industry that has as a major interest the creation of greater "lifelike" qualities in the dead, and in actuarial statistics. The military makes death impersonal, and prevalent entertainment treats death not so much as tragedy but as dramatic illusion. Concern about death has been relegated to the tabooed territory heretofore occupied by diseases like tuberculosis and cancer and the topic of sex. With the weakening of Pauline beliefs concerning the sinfulness of the body and the certainty of an afterlife, there appears to be a concomitant decrease in the ability of people to contemplate or discuss natural death.*

Nevertheless, the assaults of two World Wars together with the heritage of a potential nuclear holocaust have tended in recent years to push life's temporality more into the foreground. The existentialist movement has been particularly conspicuous in rediscovering death as a philosophical theme and problem in the twentieth century. In a sense, the history of existential philosophy in its major phases is an exegesis of man's experience of death. The image of man that emerges is that of a time-bound creature.

The existentialism of our century as expressed in the

* E. N. Jackson, "Grief and religion," in Feifel, *op. cit.;* G. Gorer, "The pornography of death," *Encounter,* 1955, 5, 49-52.

philosophies of Simmel, Sheler, Jaspers, and Heidegger has placed the experience of death near the center of its analysis of the human condition. It has accented death as a constitutive part rather than the mere end of life, and highpointed the idea that only by integrating the concept of death into the self does an authentic and genuine existence become possible. The price for denying death is undefined anxiety, self-alienation. To completely understand himself, man must confront death, become aware of personal death.

Existentialism is certainly not a psychotherapeutic technique and makes no pretenses in that direction. I feel, however, that its orientation implies consequences of a psychotherapeutic kind, concerning which May will comment in greater detail in Chapter IV.

In the limited space available to me, I wish to indicate some general findings on attitudes toward death issuing from a continuing series of investigations I am now carrying on. They will have to be considered in the nature of an interim report, tentative and subject to change. I hope, nevertheless, that they will suggest therapeutic possibilities. The results are based on four major groups: 85 mentally ill patients with a mean age of 36 years; 40 older persons with a mean age of 67 years; 85 "normals" consisting of 50 young people with a mean age of 26 years, and 35 professional persons with a mean age of 40 years; and 20 terminally ill patients with a mean age of 42 years.

In response to the question "What does death mean to you?" two outlooks dominate. One views death in philosophic vein as the natural end process of life. The other is of a religious nature, perceiving death as the dissolution of bodily life and, in reality, the beginning of a new life. This finding, in a sense, broadly mirrors the interpretation of death in the history of Western thought. From these two opposing poles, two contrasting ethics may be derived. "On the one hand the attitude toward death is the stoic or skeptic acceptance of the inevitable, or even the repression of the thought of death by life; on the other, the idealistic glorification of death is that which gives meaning to life, or is the precondition for the true life of man." * This finding underlines the profound contradiction that exists in our thinking about the problem of death. Our tradition assumes that man is both terminated by death and yet capable of continuing in some other sense beyond death. Death is seen on the one hand as a "wall," the ultimate personal disaster, and suicide as the act of a sick mind; on the other, death is regarded as a "doorway," a point in time on the way to eternity.

The *degree* of mental disturbance per se in the patients, apparently, has little effect on their over-all attitudes toward death. Neither neurosis nor psychosis produces attitudes toward death that cannot also be found in normal subjects. The emotional disturbance seemingly serves to bring *specific* attitudes more clearly to the foreground. These results reinforce the findings of Bromberg and Schilder.† Incidentally, few normal people visualize themselves as dying by means of an accident. This is in contrast to the findings for the mentally ill patients, a good proportion of whom see themselves as dying by "crashing in a plane," "being run over by a tractor," "getting shot," etc.

When asked to express their preference as to the "manner, place, and time" of death, an overwhelming majority in all the groups want to die quickly with little suffering— "peacefully in your sleep," as most put it, or "having a coronary." The remainder want to have plenty of time in order to make farewells to family and friends. "At home" and "bed" are specifically mentioned by the majority as the preferred place of death. There are, naturally, personal idiosyncrasies—"in a garden," "overlooking the ocean," "in a hammock on a spring day." About 15–20% in each group say it really does not make much difference

* H. Marcuse, "The ideology of death," in Feifel, *op. cit.*
† Bromberg and Schilder, *op. cit.*

to them where they die. One wonders whether these responses do not reflect, on some level, a reaction to our modern way of dying. No longer do most of us receive death in the privacy of our homes with family about and attending, and with a minimum of medicine to prolong life. We die in the "big" hospital with its superior facilities for providing care and alleviating pain, but also with its impersonal intravenous tubes and oxygen tents. It is as if death's reality were being obscured by making it a public event, something that befalls everyone yet no one in particular.

With reference to the time of death, most people say they want to die at night because "it would mean less trouble for everyone concerned," "little fuss." The choice of night, outside of the contemplated peaceful end of life it connotes, has many engrossing symbolic overtones. Homer in the Iliad alludes to sleep (*hypnos*) and death (*thanatos*) as twin brothers, and many of our religious prayers entwine the ideas of sleep and death. Orthodox Jews, for example, on arising from sleep in the morning thank God for having restored them to life again.

While the data were being collected and evaluated, the implication suggested itself that certain persons who fear death strongly may resort to a religious outlook in order to cope with their fears concerning death. I thought it would be fruitful to get comparative data on religious and nonreligious persons, particularly taking into account the "judgment" aspect after death as a possible important variable. The mean age of the religious group ($N = 40$) was 31.5 years; that of the nonreligious one ($N = 42$) was 34 years. The main beliefs that characterized the religious group, as distinguished from the nonreligious one, were credence in a divine purpose in the operations of the universe, in a life-after-death, and acceptance of the Bible as revealing God's truths. One should be cautious in considering the religious person as invariant; the same holds true for the nonreligious person. Individuals may derive values (sociability, emotional support, sense of belongingness, etc.) and need-satisfactions from religious membership and participation that are not necessarily related to religious belief and commitment. Also, individuals may frequently express a religious identification (tradition) without formal membership or commitment. And often, there may be a difference between the value-commitments of the individual and those required by the "official" theological structure of his particular faith.* In other words, some people may profess religious tenets but not practice them. Others may adopt religion as a kind of defense against "the slings and arrows of outrageous fortune." Then, there are those who incorporate their religious beliefs into everyday living activities. Sharper and more definitive categorization is needed in this field. For example, attitudes toward death may well vary among differing denominational groups. Our purpose, however, at this stage, was to get some general measure of fundamentalist or nonfundamentalist outlook.

The religious person, when compared to the nonreligious individual in our sample, is personally more afraid of death. The nonreligious individual fears death because "my family may not be provided for," "I want to accomplish certain things yet," "I enjoy life and want to continue on." The emphasis is on fear of discontinuance of life on earth—what is being left behind—rather than on what will happen after death. The stress for the religious person is twofold. Concern with afterlife matters—"I may go to hell," "I have sins to expiate yet"—as well as with cessation of present earthly experiences. The data indicate that even the belief in going to heaven is not a sufficient antidote for doing away with personal fear of death in some religious persons. This finding, together with the strong fear of death expressed in the older years by a substantial number of religiously inclined individuals, may reflect a

* D. J. Hager, "Religious conflict," *J. Soc. Issues,* 1956, 12, 3-11.

defensive use of religion by some of our subjects. In corresponding vein, the religious person in our studies holds a significantly more negative orientation toward the older years of life than does his nonreligious peer.

Along this line, I believe that the frenetic accent on, and continual search for, the "fountain of youth" in many segments of our society reflects, to a certain degree, anxieties concerning death. One of the reasons why we tend to reject the aged is that they remind us of death. Professional people, particularly physicians, who come in contact with chronic and terminally ill patients have noted parallel avoidant tendencies in themselves. Counterphobic attitudes toward death, for example, may be observed frequently among medical interns. Now this reaction on the part of the physician is understandable: the need to withdraw libido investment, relief from unmitigated tragedy, the reality that others may benefit more from his time, etc. But I would submit that some physicians often reject the dying patient because he reactivates or arouses their own fears about dying, that, in some, guilt feelings tied up with death wishes toward significant figures in their own lives play a role, not to speak of the wounded narcissism and lack of gratification of the physician whose function it is to save life being faced with a dying patient who represents a denial of his essential skills. I think it would prove interesting to pursue the relationship aspect of choice of occupation here, where the "saving of life" is paramount, with personal attitudes toward death in physicians. One of the unsuspected obstacles I have come up against in carrying on research in the area has been not the patient, but the physician. An hypothesis I hold, which is being continually reinforced, is that one of the major reasons certain physicians enter medicine is to master their own above-average anxieties about death.

We have been compelled, in unhealthy measure, to internalize our thoughts and feelings, fears and even hopes concerning death. One of the serious mistakes we commit, I think, in treating terminally ill patients is the erection of a psychological barrier between the living and dying. Some think and say that it is cruel and traumatic to talk to dying patients about death. Actually, my findings indicate that patients want very much to talk about their thoughts and feelings about death, but feel that we, the living, close off the avenues for their accomplishing this. A good number of them prefer honest and plain talk from physicians about the seriousness of their illness. They have a sense of being understood and helped rather than becoming frightened or panicking when they can talk about their feelings concerning death. There is truth in the idea that the unknown can be feared more than the most known, dreaded reality.

When the present investigation was initially broached, the question was raised, and rightfully so, as to the possible negative effect and "stress" aspects of the interview and testing procedures on the patients. In resulting fact, the vast majority of them showed no untoward reactions. Some of them actually thanked the project personnel for affording them the opportunity to discuss their feelings concerning death. There is almost nothing more crushing to a dying person than to feel that he has been abandoned or rejected. This realization not only removes support and prevents the patient's getting relief from the various kinds of guilt feelings that he has, but does not even permit him to make use of denial mechanisms that he may have been able to use up until then.*

Speaking of guilt, it is a startling fact that many hopelessly sick people feel guilty. This results from a number of reasons: (1) They often express the suspicion that their sickness and fate are self-inflicted and their own fault. (2) They assume, more or less, the role of the utterly dependent child. Some consciously apologize for the trouble and "fuss" they are causing. Our culture fosters a sense

* Hattie Rosenthal, "Psychotherapy for the dying," *Amer. J. Psychother.*, 1957, 11, 626-633.

of guilt in most of us when we are placed in the dependent role. (3) This is further extended in the dying person because of his feelings that he is forcing the living about him to face the necessity and finality of death, for which they will hate him. (4) Closely allied to this is the sick person's dim awareness of his envy of those who remain alive and of the wish, rarely entering consciousness, that the spouse, parent, child, or friend die in his stead. There is the thought that it may be this wish, in part, that breaks into action in those cases of seriously ill people who kill not only themselves but family and neighbors as well.*

The living respond with guilt of their own—for being alive and seeing someone else die, and, perhaps, for even wishing that the dying person hurry along on his way. In truth, most healthy people feel anxious and guilty at seeing someone else die. Being faced directly with the existential fact of death seems to cast a blight on ego functioning.

Yet, we are aware that human maturity brings along with it a recognition of limit, which is a notable advance in self-knowledge. In a certain sense, the willingness to die appears as a necessary condition of life. We are not altogether free in any deed as long as we are commanded by an inescapable will to live. In this context, the everyday risks of living, e.g., driving downtown, taking an airplane trip to Cincinnati, losing one's guard in sleep become almost forms of extravagant folly. Life is not genuinely our own until we can renounce it.† Montaigne has penetratingly remarked that "only the man who no longer fears death has ceased to be a slave."

Clinical observation prompts the reflection that for many individuals perception of death from a temporal distance and when it is personally near may be two quite different matters. Also, knowledge of the "external" degree of

* G. J. Aronson, "Treatment of the dying person," in Feifel, *op. cit.*

† W. E. Hocking, *The meaning of immortality in human experience* (New York: Harper, 1957).

threat alone appears to be an insufficient base on which to predict with any certainty how a person will react to it. Information that you are to die in the near future does not necessarily constitute an *extreme* stress situation for specific individuals. The person's character structure—the type of person he is—may sometimes be more important than the death-threat stimulus itself in determining reactions. In ongoing work, we hope to scrutinize closely the existing relationships here, i.e., relating attitudes toward death to the *kind* of person who has them.

My own tentative thesis is that types of reaction to impending death are a function of interweaving factors. I strongly support the outlook of Beigler* here. Some of the more significant ones tentatively appear to be: (1) the psychologic maturity of the individual; (2) kind of coping techniques available to him; (3) influence of such varying frames of reference as religious orientation, age, sex; (4) severity of the organic process; and (5) the attitudes of the physician and other significant persons in the patient's world.

The research in progress reinforces the thinking that death can mean different things to different people. Even in a rather narrowly defined cultural group, the non-homogeneous psychological quality of fear of death becomes evident.† Death is a multifaceted symbol whose specific meaning depends on the nature and fortunes of the individual's development and cultural context. "Death is terrible to Cicero, desirable to Cato, and indifferent to Socrates."

One *leitmotif,* however, that persists in coming to the fore when one works in the area is that the crisis is often not the fact of oncoming death per se, of man's unsur-

* J. Beigler, "Anxiety as an aid in the prognostication of impending death," *A.M.A. Arch. Neurol. Psychiat.*, 1957, 77, 171-177.

† G. Murphy, "Discussion," in Feifel, *op. cit.*

mountable finiteness, but rather the waste of limited years, the unassayed tasks, the locked opportunities, the talents withering in disuse, the avoidable evils that have been done. The tragedy which is underlined is that man dies prematurely and without dignity, that death has not become really "his own."

To conclude: A man's birth is an uncontrollable event in his life, but the manner of his departure from life bears a definite relation to his philosophy of life and death. We are mistaken in considering death a purely biologic event.* Life is not comprehended truly or lived fully unless the idea of death is grappled with honestly.

There is a pressing need for more reliable information and systematic, controlled study in the field. This is an area in which theoretical formulations have not been lagging behind an accumulating body of descriptive and empirical data. Research on the meaning of death and dying can enhance our understanding of the individual's behavior and yield an additional entryway to an analysis of cultures.

Let me not be misunderstood. I do not hold that the human condition is fully described by care and anxiety, dread and death. Joy, love, happiness provide clues just as valid to reality and being.† As Gardner Murphy‡ has discerningly pointed out, it is far from being established that *all* facing of death necessarily represents gains in mental health. In some studies of pilots during World War II,§ it was found that those who did not break down psychologically retained, in the moments of most extreme

---

ᵏ K. R. Eissler, *The psychiatrist and the dying patient* (New York: International Univ. Press, 1955).

† J. Taubes, "Mortality and anxiety." Unpublished paper, 1956.

‡ G. Murphy, *op. cit.*

§ R. R. Grinker and J. P. Spiegel, *Men under stress* (Philadelphia: Blakiston, 1945).

danger, the illusion of invulnerability. Apparently, there is a need to face death and also a need to face away from it.*

My point is that it is a much needed step forward for psychology to recognize that the concept of death represents a psychological and social fact of substantial import and that the dying words attributed to Goethe—"More light"—are particularly appropriate to the field under discussion.

* G. Murphy, *op. cit.*

CHAPTER IV

ROLLO MAY

Existential Bases of Psychotherapy

There are several endeavors in this country to systematize psychoanalytic and psychotherapeutic theory in terms of forces, dynamisms, and energies. The existential approach is the exact opposite of these attempts. It holds, as I have said in Chapter I, that our science must be relevant to the distinctive characteristics of what we seek to study, in this case the human being. We do not deny dynamisms and forces; that would be nonsense. But we hold that they have meaning only in the context of the existing, living being—if you will permit a technical word, only in the *ontological* context.

I propose, then, that we take the one real datum that we have in the therapeutic situation, namely, the existing person sitting in the consulting room with a therapist. Let us

75

ask: What are the essential characteristics which constitute this patient as an existing person, which constitute this self as a self? I wish to propose six characteristics, which I shall call principles, that I find in my work as a psychotherapist. They can as well be called *ontological characteristics*. Though these are the product of a good deal of thought and experience with many cases, I shall illustrate them with episodes from the case of Mrs. Hutchens.*

First, Mrs. Hutchens, like every existing person, is centered in herself, and an attack on this center is an attack on her existence itself. This is a characteristic that we human beings share with all living beings; it is self-evident in animals and plants. I never cease to marvel how, whenever we cut the top off a pine tree on our farm in New Hampshire, the tree sends up a new branch from heaven knows where to become a new center. But our principle has a particular relevance to human beings and gives a basis for the understanding of sickness and health, neurosis and mental health. Neurosis is not to be seen as a deviation from our particular theories of what a person should be. *Is not neurosis, rather, precisely the method the individual uses to preserve his own center, his own existence?* His symptoms are ways of shrinking the range of his world (so graphically shown in Mrs. Hutchens' inability to let herself talk) in order that the centeredness of his existence may be protected from threat, a way of blocking off aspects of the environment so that he may then be adequate to the remainder.

Mrs. Hutchens had gone to another therapist for half a dozen sessions a month before she came to me. He told her, in an apparently ill-advised effort to reassure her, that she was too proper, too controlled. She reacted with great upset and immediately broke off the treatment. Now, technically he was entirely correct; existentially he was entirely wrong. What he did not see, in my judgment, was this very proper-

* This patient and her presenting symptoms were briefly discussed in Chapter I, page 25.

ness, this overcontrol, far from being things that Mrs.
Hutchens wanted to get over, were part of her desperate
attempt to preserve what precarious center she had. As
though she were saying, "If I opened up, if I communi-
cated, I would lose what little space in life I have." We
see here, incidentally, how inadequate is the definition of
neurosis as a failure of adjustment. *An adjustment is
exactly what neurosis is; and that is just its trouble*. It is a
necessary adjustment by which centeredness can be preserved; a way of accepting *non-being,* if I may use this
term, in order that some little *being* may be preserved. And
in most cases it is a boon when this adjustment breaks
down.

This is the only thing we can assume about Mrs.
Hutchens, or about any patient, when she comes in: she,
like all living beings, requires centeredness, and this has
broken down. At a cost of considerable turmoil she has
taken steps, that is, come for help. Our second principle,
thus, is: every existing person *has the character of self-
affirmation, the need to preserve its centeredness*. The particular name we give this self-affirmation in human beings
is "courage." Paul Tillich's emphasis on the "courage to
be" is very important, cogent, and fertile for psychotherapy
at this point. He insists that in man, being is never given
automatically, as it is in plants and animals, but depends
upon the individual's courage, and without courage one
loses being. This makes courage itself a necessary ontological corollary. By this token, I as a therapist place great importance upon expressions of the patients which have to
do with willing, decisions, choice. I never let such little
remarks the patient may make as "maybe I can," "perhaps
I can try" slip by without my making sure he knows I
have heard him. It is only a half truth to say that the will
is the product of the wish; I emphasize rather the truth
that the wish can never come out in its real power except
with will.

Now as Mrs. Hutchens talks hoarsely, she looks at me

with an expression of mingled fear and hope. Obviously a relation not only exists between us here, but has already existed in anticipation in the waiting room and ever since she thought of coming. She is struggling with the possibility of participating with me. Our third principle is, thus: *all existing persons have the need and possibility of going out from their centeredness to participate in other beings.* This always involves risk; if the organism goes out too far, it loses its own centeredness, its identity—a phenomenon which can easily be seen in the biological world. If the neurotic is so afraid of loss of his own conflicted center that he refuses to go out and holds back in rigidity and lives in narrowed reactions and shrunken world space, his growth and development are blocked. This is the pattern in neurotic repressions and inhibitions, the common neurotic forms in Freud's day. But it may well be in our day of conformity and the outerdirected man, that the most common neurotic pattern takes the opposite form, namely, the dispersing of one's self in participation and identification with others until one's own being is emptied.

At this point we see the rightful emphasis of Martin Buber in one sense and Harry Stack Sullivan in another, that the human being cannot be understood as a self if participation is omitted. Indeed, if we are successful in our search for these ontological principles of the existing person, it should be true that the omission of any one of the six would mean that we do not then have a human being.

Our fourth principle is: *the subjective side of centeredness is awareness.* Such awareness is present in forms of life other than human; it is certainly observable in animals. Howard Liddell has pointed out how the seal in its natural habitat lifts its head every ten seconds even during sleep to survey the horizon lest an Eskimo hunter with poised bow and arrow sneak up on it. This awareness of threats to being in animals, Liddell calls *vigilance,* and he identifies it as the primitive, simple counterpart in animals of what in human beings becomes anxiety.

Our first four characteristic principles are shared by our existing person with all living beings; they are biological levels in which human beings participate. The fifth principle refers now to a distinctively human characteristic: self-consciousness. *The uniquely human form of awareness is self-consciousness.* Awareness and consciousness should not be identified. We associate awareness, as Liddell indicates, with vigilance. This is supported by the derivation of the term "aware." It comes from the Anglo-Saxon *gewaer, waer,* meaning knowledge of external dangers and threats. Its cognates are *beware* and *wary.* Awareness certainly is what is going on in an individual's neurotic reaction to threat, in, for example, Mrs. Hutchens' experience in the first hours that I am also a threat to her.

Consciousness, however, is not simply my awareness of threat from the world but *my capacity to know myself as the one being threatened, my experience of myself as the subject who has a world.* Consciousness, to use Kurt Goldstein's terms, is man's capacity to transcend the immediate concrete situation, to live in terms of the possible; and it underlies the human capacity to use abstractions and universals, to have language and symbols. This capacity for consciousness underlies the wide range of possibility which man has in relating to his world, and it constitutes the foundation of psychological freedom. Thus, human freedom has its ontological base and I believe must be assumed in all psychotherapy.

In his book *The Phenomenon of Man,* the paleontologist Pierre Teilhard de Chardin brilliantly describes how awareness is present, including the form of tropism, in all forms of evolutionary life from amoeba to man. But in man a new function arises, namely this self-consciousness. Teilhard de Chardin undertakes to demonstrate something that I have always believed, that when a new function emerges, the whole previous pattern of the organism changes. The total gestalt shifts; thereafter the organism can be understood only in terms of the new function. That is to say, it is only a half truth to hold that the organism is to be understood in terms of the simpler elements below it on the e olutionary scale; it is just as true that every new function forms a new complexity which conditions all the simpler elements in this organism. Thus, *the simple can be u derstood only in terms of the more complex.*

This is what self-consciousness does in man. All the simpler biological functions must now be understood in terms of this new function. No one would, of course, deny for a moment the old functions, or anything in biology which man shares with less complex organisms. Take sexuality, for example, which we obviously share with all mammals. But given self-consciousness, sex becomes a new gestalt, as is demonstrated in therapy all the time. Sexual impulses are always, then, conditioned by the *person* of the partner; what we think of the other male or female, in reality or fantasy or even repressed fantasy, can never be ruled out. The fact that the subjective person of the other to whom we relate sexually makes least difference in *neurotic* sexuality, say in patterns of compulsive sex or prostitution, only proves our point the more firmly, for such requires precisely the blocking off, the checking out, the distorting of self-consciousness. Thus, when we talk of sexuality in terms of sexual objects, as Kinsey does, we may garner interesting and useful statistics; but we simply are not talking about human sexuality.

Nothing in what I am saying here should be taken as antibiological in the slightest; on the contrary, I think it is only from this approach that we *can* understand human biology without distorting it. As Kierkegaard aptly put it, "The natural law is as valid as ever." I argue only against the uncritical acceptance of the assumption that the organism is to be understood only in terms of those elements below it on the evolutionary scale, an acceptance which has led us to overlook the self-evident truth that what makes a horse a horse are not the elements it shares with the dog but what constitutes distinctively, "horse." Now, *what we are dealing with in neurosis are those character-istics and functions that are distinctively human.* It is these that have gone awry in disturbed patients. The condition for these functions is self-consciousness—which accounts for what Freud rightly discovered, that the neurotic pattern is characterized by repression and blocking off of conscious-ness.

It is the task of the therapist, therefore, not only to help the patient become aware, but even more significantly, to help him *transmute this awareness into consciousness.* Awareness is his knowing that something is threatening from outside in his world—a condition that may, as in paranoids and their neurotic equivalents, be correlated with a good deal of acting-out behavior. But self-conscious-ness puts this awareness on a quite different level; it is the patient's seeing that *he is the one who is threatened,* that he is the being who stands in this world which threatens, that he is the subject who *has* a world. And this gives him the possibility of *in-sight,* of "inward sight," of seeing the world and his problems in relation to himself. And thus it gives him the possibility of doing something about them.

To come back to our too-long silent patient: After about twenty-five hours of therapy Mrs. Hutchens had the fol-lowing dream. She was searching room by room for a baby in an unfinished house at an airport. She thought the baby belonged to someone else, but the other person might let her take it. Now it seemed that she had put the baby in a pocket of her robe (or her mother's robe), and she was seized with anxiety that it would be smothered. Much to her joy, she found that the baby was still alive. Then she had a strange thought, "Shall I kill it?"

The house was at the airport where she, at about the age of twenty, had learned to fly solo, a very important act of self-affirmation and independence from her parents.

The baby was associated with her youngest son, whom she regularly identified with herself. Permit me to omit the ample associative evidence that convinced both her and me that the baby stood for herself, and specifically for consciousness of herself. The dream is an expression of the emergence and growth of self-consciousness, a consciousness that she is not yet sure is hers, and a consciousness that she considers killing in the dream.

About six years before her therapy, Mrs. Hutchens had left the religious faith of her parents, to which, by way of them, she had had a very authoritarian relation. She had then joined a church of her own belief. But she had never dared tell her parents of this. Instead, when they came to visit, she attended their church in great tension lest one of her children let the secret out. After about thirty-five sessions, when she was considering writing her parents to tell them of this change of faith, she had, over a period of two weeks, spells of partially fainting in my office. She would become suddenly weak, her face would go white, she would feel empty and "like water inside" and would have to lie down for a few moments on the couch. In retrospect, she called these spells "grasping for oblivion."

She then wrote her parents informing them once and for all of her change in faith and assuring them it would do no good to try to dominate her. The following session, she asked in considerable anxiety whether I thought she would go psychotic. I responded that whereas anyone of us might at some time have such an episode, I saw no more reason why she should than any of the rest of us; and I asked whether her fear of going psychotic was not rather anxiety arising out of her standing against her parents, as though genuinely being herself, she felt to be tantamount to going crazy. I have noted several times, it may be remarked, that patients experience this anxiety at being one's self as tantamount to psychosis. This is not surprising, for consciousness of one's own desires and affirming them involves accepting one's originality and uniqueness, and it implies that one must be prepared not only to be isolated from those parental figures upon whom one has been dependent, but at that instant to stand alone in the entire psychic universe as well.

We see the profound conflicts of the emergence of self-consciousness in three vivid ways in Mrs. Hutchens, whose chief symptom, interestingly enough, was the denial of that uniquely human capacity based on consciousness, talking. These conflicts are shown in: (1) the temptation to kill the baby; (2) the grasping at oblivion by fainting, as though she were saying, "If only I did not have to be conscious, I would escape this terrible problem of telling my parents"; and (3) the psychosis anxiety.

We now come to the sixth and last characteristic of the existing person: *anxiety*. Anxiety is the state of the human being in the struggle against that which would destroy his being. It is, in Tillich's phrase, the state of a being in conflict with nonbeing, a conflict which Freud mythologically pictured in his powerful and important symbol of the death instinct. One wing of this struggle will always be against something outside one's self; but even more portentous and significant for psychotherapy is the inner side of the battle, which we saw in Mrs. Hutchens, namely, the conflict within the person as he confronts the choice of whether and how far he will stand against his own being, his own potentialities.

Thus, we take very seriously this temptation to kill the baby, or kill her own consciousness, as expressed in these forms by Mrs. Hutchens. We neither water it down by calling it "neurotic" and the product merely of sickness, nor do we slough over it by reassuring her, "Okay, but you don't need to do it." If we did these, we would be helping her adjust at the price of surrendering a portion of her existence, that is, her opportunity for fuller independence. The self-confrontation which is involved in the acceptance of self-consciousness is anything but simple: it involves, to identify some of the elements, accepting of the hatred of the past, her mother's against her and hers of her mother; accepting her present motives of hatred and destruction; cutting through rationalizations and illusions about her behavior and motives, and the acceptance of the responsibility and aloneness which this implies; the giving up of childhood omnipotence, and acceptance of the fact that although she can never have absolute certainty about her choices, she must choose anyway.

But all these specific points, easy enough to understand in themselves, must be seen in the light of the fact that *consciousness itself implies always the possibility of turning against one's self, denying one's self.* The tragic nature of human existence inheres in the fact that consciousness itself involves the possibility and temptation at every instant to kill itself. Dostoevski and our other existential forebears were not indulging in poetic hyperbole or expressing the aftereffects of too much vodka the night before when they wrote of the agonizing burden of freedom.

I trust that the fact that existential psychotherapy places emphasis on these tragic aspects of life does not at all give the impression that it is pessimistic. Quite the contrary. The confronting of genuine tragedy is a highly cathartic experience psychically, as Aristotle and others through history have reminded us. Tragedy is inseparably connected with man's dignity and grandeur and is the accompaniment, as illustrated in the dramas of Oedipus and Orestes, ad infinitum, of the human being's moment of great insight.

In my judgment, the analysis of characteristics of the existing being, these ontological characteristics that I have tried to point toward, can give us a structural base for our psychotherapy. It can also give us a base for a science of man that will not fragmentize and destroy man's humanity as it studies him.

CHAPTER V

CARL R. ROGERS

Two Divergent Trends

During the course of the convention at which these papers
were initially read, I was called upon to comment on two
presentations, one involving a general theory of psychotherapy based on learning theory, and the other the existential point of view in psychology and psychotherapy that
now appears in the earlier chapters of this book. These
two presentations symbolize in an interesting way two
strong currents in present-day American psychology, currents that at the moment seem irreconcilable because we
have not yet developed the larger frame of reference that
would contain them both. Because my own interest is
primarily in psychotherapy, I am going to limit myself here
to a discussion of these trends as they appear in this field.

The "Objective" Trend

On the one hand our devotion to rigorous hard-headedness in psychology, to reductionist theories, to operational definitions, to experimental procedures leads us to understand psychotherapy in purely objective rather than subjective terms. Thus we can conceptualize therapy as being simply the operant conditioning of the client. The therapist reinforces, by appropriate simple measures, those statements expressing feelings, or those which report dream content, or those which express hostility, or those which show a positive self-concept. Impressive evidence has been produced indicating that such reinforcement does increase the type of expression reinforced. Hence the road to improvement in therapy, in this view, is to select more wisely the elements to reinforce, to have more clearly in mind the behaviors toward which we wish to shape our clients. The problem is not different in kind from Skinner's shaping of the behavior of his pigeons toward ping-pong playing.

Another variant of this general trend is what is known as the learning-theory approach to psychotherapy, which exists in several forms. Those S-R bonds are identified that are anxiety creating or that have caused difficulties in adjustment. These are labeled, and their origin and effects are interpreted and explained to the subject. Reconditioning or counterconditioning is then utilized so that the individual acquires a new, more healthy, and more socially useful response to the same stimulus that originally caused difficulty.

This whole trend has behind it the weight of current attitudes in American psychology. As I see them, these attitudes include such themes as: "Away from the philosophical and the vague. On toward the concrete, the operationally defined, the specific." "Away from anything which looks within. Our behaviors and our selves are nothing but objects molded and shaped by conditioning circumstances. The future is determined by the past." "Since no one is free, we had better manipulate the behavior of others in an intelligent fashion, for the general good." (How unfree individuals can choose what they wish to do, and choose to manipulate others, is never made clear.) "The way to do is to *do,* quite obviously." "The way to understand is from the outside."

The "Existential" Trend

Logical and natural as this trend may be, suited as it is to the temper of our culture, it is not the only trend that is evident. In Europe, which has not become so involved in scientism, and increasingly in this country, other voices are saying: "This tunnel vision of behavior is *not* adequate to the whole range of *human* phenomena." One of these voices is Abraham Maslow. Another is Rollo May. Another is Gordon Allport. There are an increasing number of others. I would like, if I may, to place myself in this group. These psychologists insist, in a variety of ways, that they are concerned with the whole spectrum of human behavior and that *human* behavior is, in some significant ways, something more than the behavior of our laboratory animals.

To illustrate this in the realm of psychotherapy, I should like to cite, very briefly, some of my own experience. I started from a thoroughly objective point of view. Psychotherapeutic treatment involved the diagnosis and analysis of the client's difficulties, the cautious interpretation and explanation to the client of the causes of his difficulties, and a re-educative process focused by the clinician upon the specific causal elements. Gradually I observed that I was more effective if I could create a psychological climate in which the client could undertake these functions himself—exploring, analyzing, understanding, and trying new solutions to his problems. During more recent years, I have been forced to recognize that the most important ingredient in creating this climate is that I should be *real*. I have come to realize that only when I am able to be a transparently real person, and am so perceived by my client, can he discover what is real in him. Then my empathy and acceptance can be effective. When I fal short in therapy, it is when I am unable to be what I deeply am. The essence of therapy, as I see it carried on by myself and by others, is a meeting of two *persons* in which the therapist is openly and freely himself and evidences this perhaps most fully when he can freely and acceptantly enter into the world of the other. Thus, borrowing from some ancient phrases, I am inclined to say, "The way to do is to *be*." "The way to understand is from within."

The result of this kind of a relationship has been wel described by May. The client finds himself confirmed (to use Buber's term) not only in what he is, but in his potentialities. He can affirm himself, fearfully to be sure, as a separate, unique person. He can become the architect of his own future through the functioning of his consciousness. What this means is that because he is more open to his experience, he can permit himself to live symbolically in terms of all the possibilities. He can acceptantly live out, in his thoughts and feelings, the creative urges within himself, the destructive tendencies he finds within, the challenge of growth, the challenge of death. He can face, in his consciousness, what it will mean to him to *be*, and what it will mean to not be. He becomes an autonomous human person, able to be what he is and to choose his course. This is the outcome of therapy, as seen by this second trend.

Two Modes of Science

We may well ask how these different trends in therapy could come about—the one symbolized by Dollard, Miller, Rotter, Wolpe, Bergman, and others, the second by May,

Maslow, myself, and others. I believe the divergence arises in part out of a differential conception of and use of science. To put it in oversimplified fashion, the learning theorist says, "We know much about how animals learn. Therapy is learning. Therefore effective therapy will be composed of what we know about animal learning." This is a perfectly legitimate use of science, projecting known findings into new and unknown fields.

The second group approaches the problem differently. These individuals are interested in observing the underlying order in therapeutic events. They say, "Some efforts to be therapeutic, to bring about constructive change, are effective; others are not. We find that there are certain characteristics that differentiate the two classes. We find, for example, that in the helpful relationships, it is likely that the therapist functions as a real person, interacting with his real feelings. In the less helpful relationships, we frequently find that the therapist functions as an intelligent manipulator, rather than as his real self." Here too is a perfectly legitimate concept of science, the detecting of the order which is inherent in any given series of events. I submit that this second conception is more likely to discover the uniquely human aspects of therapy.

Empirical Method as a Rapprochement

I have tried to sketch briefly these two divergent currents, whose advocates often find communication difficult because their differences are so great. Perhaps one function I can serve is to indicate that scientific method itself provides a basis for rapprochement. Let me be more specific.

As May has stated his six principles, they must be abhorrent to many American psychologists because they sound so vague, so philosophical, so untestable. Yet I found no difficulty at all in deducing testable hypotheses from his principles. Here are some examples.

From his first principle: The more the *self* of the person is threatened, the more he will exhibit defensive neurotic behavior.

The more the self of the person is threatened the more his ways of being and behavior will become constricted.

From his principle number two: The more the self is free from threat, the more the individual will exhibit self-affirming behaviors.

From principle number three, the hypothesis is more complex, but still crudely testable: The more the individual experiences a climate free from threat to self, the more he will exhibit the need for, and the actualization of, participant behavior.

From principle number six: A specific anxiety will be resolved only if the client loses the fear of *being* the specific potentiality regarding which he has been anxious.

Perhaps I have said enough to suggest that our positivist tradition of operational definitions and empirical research may be helpful in investigating the truth of the ontological principles of therapy set forth by May, the principles of personality dynamics implicit in Maslow's remarks, and even the effects of different perceptions of death as set forth by Feifel. In the long run, it is likely, as Maslow hopes, that the involvement of psychological science in these subtle, subjective, and value-permeated fields will in itself bring about the next step in the theory of science.

An Example

To illustrate more clearly the way in which research may clarify some of these issues, let me leap into one of the most controversial differences, and illuminate it from some studies out of the past. One of the elements of existential thinking most shocking to conventional American psychologists is that it speaks as if man were free and responsible, as though choice constituted the core of his existence. This has been evident in our speakers today.

Feifel says, "Life is not genuinely our own until we can renounce it." Maslow points out that psychologists have been dodging the problem of responsibility and the place of courage in the personality. May speaks of "the agonizing burden of freedom" and the choice between being one's self or denying one's self. Certainly to many psychologists today these can never be issues with which the *science* of psychology can be concerned. They are simply speculations.

Yet bearing on precisely this point, I should like to bring in some research of a number of years ago. W. L. Kell, doing his graduate work under my supervision, chose to study the factors that would predict the behavior of adolescent delinquents.* He made careful objective ratings of the family climate, the educational experiences, the neighborhood and cultural influences, the social experiences, the health history, the hereditary background of each delinquent. These factors were rated as to their favorableness for normal development, on a continuum from elements destructive of the child's welfare and inimical to healthy development, to elements highly conducive to healthy development. Almost as an afterthought, a rating was also made of the degree of self-understanding, because it was felt that although this was not one of the primary conditioning factors, it might play some part in predicting future behavior. This was essentially a rating of the degree to which the individual was objective and realistic regarding himself and his situation, whether he was emotionally acceptant of the facts in himself and in his environment.

These ratings, on 75 delinquents, were compared with ratings of their behavior two to three years after the initial study. It was expected that the ratings on family climate and social experience with peers would be the best predictors of later behavior. To our amazement, the degree of self-understanding was much the best predictor, correlating

---

* C. R. Rogers, W. L. Kell, and H. McNeil, "The role of self-understanding in the prediction of behavior," *Jour. Consult. Psychol.*, 1948, *12*, 174-186.

.84 with later behavior, whereas quality of social experience correlated .55, and family climate .36. We simply were not prepared to believe these findings and laid the study on the shelf until it could be replicated. Later it was replicated on a new group of 76 cases, and all the essential findings were confirmed, though not quite so strikingly. Furthermore, the findings stood up even in detailed analysis. When we examined only the delinquents who came from the most unfavorable homes and who remained in those homes, it was still true that their future behavior was best predicted not by the unfavorable conditioning they were receiving in their home environment, but by the degree of realistic understanding of themselves and their environment that they possessed.

Here, it seems to me, is an empirical definition of what constitutes "freedom" in the sense in which Dr. May has used that term. As these delinquents were able to accept into consciousness all the facts regarding themselves and their situation, they were free to live out all the possibilities symbolically and to choose the most satisfying course of action. But those delinquents who were unable to accept reality into consciousness were compelled by the external circumstances of their lives to continue in a deviant course of behavior, unsatisfying in the long run. They were unfree. This study gives, I believe, some empirical meaning to Dr. May's statement that the "capacity for consciousness . . . constitutes the base of psychological freedom."

I have tried to point up the two diverging ways in which psychotherapy may be carried on. On the one hand, there is the strictly objective approach—nonhumanistic, impersonal, rationally based on knowledge of animal learning. On the other hand, there is the kind of approach suggested in the papers on this program, a humanistic, personal encounter in which the concern is with an "existing, becoming, emerging, experiencing being."

I have proposed that an empirical research method can

study the effectiveness of each of these approaches. I have tried to indicate that the subtlety and subjective qualities of the second approach are not a barrier to its objective investigation. And I am sure that it has been clear that in my judgment the warm, subjective, human encounter of two persons is more effective in facilitating change than is the most precise set of techniques growing out of learning theory or operant conditioning.

CHAPTER VI

GORDON W. ALLPORT

Comment on Earlier Chapters

Although each paper merits extended discussion, I shall be forced to limit myself to a brief comment on four issues that seem to be especially crucial:

Maslow asks: "What's in European existentialism for the American psychologist?" In a moment, I shall offer my own answer to this question—a paraphrase, I think, of Maslow's answer.

But, first, if we are candid, most of us will admit that we are repelled by much of the writing and theorizing of our European colleagues. Some of it seems to us turgid, verbalistic, and reckless. A few of the ideas are as bright and as illuminating as the dawn; but often these are then drowned in a sea of darkness. The early chapters of

Existence (17) were the dawn to me, later chapters sheer darkness.

The preceding chapters show very well how American psychology sets about recasting imported ideas, bringing order, clarity, and empirical testing to bear on them. American psychology has had few, if any, original theories of its own; but it has performed a great service in extending and rendering more precise the contributions of Pavlov, Binet, Freud, Rorschach, and others. Now I predict we can perform a like service for Heidegger, Jaspers, and Binswanger. The papers of this symposium have already taken sturdy strides in this direction. In particular, the comments by Rogers show how American psychology will seek to recast existential dogma into testable propositions.

On the positive side, Maslow finds several gains in existentialism. The movement causes us, for example, to give new weight to the concepts of identity, choice, responsibility, futurity; and it presses us toward improved methods of person perception, away from brittle, dreambook techniques and overintellectualization, and above all toward devices for the idiographic study of the unique individual. I would venture to sum up Maslow's points by saying: *Existentialism deepens the concepts that define the human condition.* In so doing, it prepares the way (for the first time) for a *psychology of mankind.* Let me explain what I mean.

A series of facts unites mankind—all mankind. The human being is born of a father and mother, ordinarily conceived and nurtured in love. He pursues certain biological goals; but he also pursues other goals which require him to establish his own identity, to take responsibility, to satisfy his curiosity concerning the meaning of life. He usually falls in love and procreates. He always dies alone. Along the way, he experiences anxiety, longing, pain, and pleasure.

This series of events is universal; but psychology has never before gone about its task with this sharpened perspective. For this reason our store of concepts and methods and our points of emphasis are defective in handling many items in this series. Existentialism invites us to fashion a universal psychology of mankind.

One of the neglected items is *death*, the subject of the excellent paper by Feifel. It strikes me as outrageous that he feels compelled to title it "Death—A Relevant Variable in Psychology." Of course it is a relevant variable. Why is it that at this late date we still need to be persuaded?

As Feifel points out, a person's philosophy of death is a large part of his philosophy of life. Some regard death as terrible, some as desirable, some as indifferent. Because individual variations are subtle and numerous, why have we up to now not included outlook on death in our studies of personality and in our therapeutic horizons? As Feifel also points out, Freud's dogma of the "death wish" has proved to be sterile. Far more promising are Feifel's own beginnings of empirical investigation. Instead of assuming, as Freud does, that all men "seek" death, we shall soon have a more discriminating and enlightening report on the matter.

I should like, however, to ask Feifel to study more closely the variable of religion. He reports tentatively that religious people in general seem to be more afraid of death. But he also properly hints that there are more ways than one of being religious. When he looks more closely into the relationship, I predict that he will find two opposite trends. People whose religious values are "intrinsic," that is to say, comprehensive and integrative in their lives (true ends-in-themselves), will be less afraid of death. By contrast, those with "extrinsic" religious values (defensive, escapist, ethnocentric) will be more afraid. My prediction here follows our discovery that ethnic prejudice is positively associated with an extrinsic type of religion, whereas the intrinsic type makes for tolerance and universalism of outlook.

The third issue is of a different kind. Both Maslow and Feifel find European existentialism too preoccupied with dread, anguish, despair, and "nausea," the only remedy for which is a stiff upper lip! The beatnik aspect of existentialism is European, not American, in flavor.

Trends in American existentialism will be (and are) far more optimistic. Sartre says there is "no exit." One is reminded of Epictetus the Stoic, who long ago wrote, "So your nose runs? What then, you fool, be glad you have a sleeve to wipe it on." Can anyone picture Carl Rogers offering such counsel?

American patients suffer as deeply and, as Maslow says, are as distressed by the shallowness of their lives as are European patients. Yet the emphasis on resignation, acceptance, even on the "courage to be" seems more European than American. Viktor Frankl, whose recent book, *From Death Camp to Existentialism*, strikes me as the wisest elementary book on the subject, holds out little hope beyond acceptance of responsibility and the discovery of a meaning in suffering. American movements of the quasi-existential order (client-centered, growth, self-actualization, and ego therapies) are more optimistic in their orientation.

Finally, what I consider to be the central theoretical issue is raised by May's stimulating Chapter IV. He seems to suggest that phenomenology (that is, taking the client's own view of himself as a unique being-in-the-world) is the first stage of therapy—and perhaps only the first stage. (I am reminded of Robert MacLeod's similar claim a few years ago, that phenomenology is a good starting point, but poor end point, for social psychology.)

Now May admits that true existentialists would go further. They would say that if we understand the *what* in its full reality and richness, the *why* will be included. But the case of Mrs. Hutchens, presented by Dr. May, does not follow this theoretical orientation. True, he depicts carefully her image of herself in a threatening world.

But his therapy relies heavily on psychoanalytic techniques. Her problem is conceptualized in the familiar Freudian manner involving the theory of reaction formation, displacement, sublimation, and projection. Mrs. Hutchens' unconscious is filled with Freudian, not existential, furniture.

The theoretical issue is this: May not the patient's distorted view of the world sometimes constitute his ultimate problem? May not the effective motives of the life lie wholly in the disordered outlook? (I have in mind a recently retired submarine commander who has an habitually domineering and impatient manner. He believes that others should obey him instantly and is accordingly sour and disordered in his perception of others. I doubt that his problem lies back in his childhood. Because of circumstances, he has evolved a distorted view of his social relationships—and *that* is his problem.)

In short, existentialists would no doubt claim that sometimes what we call "symptoms" are in fact the ultimate problem. More and more we are coming to ascribe motivational force to cognitive conditions (cf. Festinger's "cognitive dissonance" and Bartlett's "effort after meaning"). Instead of the patient's phenomenological view offering us only the first stage, perhaps it constitutes the whole problem; it is ultimate as well as preliminary for therapy.

Let me hasten to add that I do not claim that this condition always holds. Repressions may have to be cleared up; unconscious hostilities may have to be made conscious. Therapy may have to employ conventional depth techniques.

All that I am saying is that our symposium has raised what to me is the fundamental issue in motivational theory. May not (sometimes at least) an acquired world-outlook constitute the central motive of a life and, if it is disordered, the ultimate therapeutic problem? May not a person's philosophy of life, here and now, be a functionally autonomous motive? Need we always dig deeper than the presenting phenomenology?

My own view is that psychology urgently needs to make a distinction between lives in which the existential layer is, in effect, the whole of the personality, and other lives in which it is a mere mask for the rumblings of the unconscious.

JOSEPH LYONS

*A Bibliographic Introduction to Phenomenology and Existentialism**

This bibliography provides an introduction to this field by emphasizing writings in English in which phenomenological or existentialist conceptions are applied explicitly to issues in the field of psychology. The area thus defined is, however, not easily demarcated. I have ruled out: (a) the bulk of writings that have not been translated into English; (b) works that belong entirely within fields other than psychology, such as theology or literary criticism; (c) sources and materials that are of interest primarily for historical reasons, as for example the writings of St. Augustine, Pascal, and other so-called precursors of con-

* Parts of this material appeared under the title "An annotated bibliography on phenomenology and existentialism" in *Psychological Reports,* 1959, 5, 613-631 (© Southern Universities Press 1959.)

temporary existentialist thinking; (d) a large number of studies by such men as Rubin, Katz, Heider, Goldstein, and Schachtel, as not explicitly demonstrating the application of phenomenology to psychological problems, although they were all greatly influenced by Husserl's ideas and methods; (e) the contributions of many psychologists whose thinking—in my own view, at least—often strikingly parallels that of the phenomenologists but who have never publicly identified themselves as such; (f) examples of related orientations, in particular the Thomistic and classical *Gestalttheorie;* and (g) dissertations, abstracts, and items from newsletters, which do not form part of the corpus of permanent psychological literature. In the case of the large number of recent expository texts on existentialism, I include a mere sampling, chosen by the criteria of soundness, thoroughness, and relevance for psychologists. In short, I have tried to compile an academically practical listing in an area in which the great need is still for basic knowledge.

Some of the items will be recognized as critical of the phenomenological or existential orientation but are included as enlightening or edifying for psychologists. Although I have tried to keep the effect of my own bias to a minimum and have even included some material which might be called phenomenological only by grace of a laxity in terminology, the reader will surely recognize my preferences, as for example in the space given to the works of Straus and Sartre. My annotations are, however, noncritical in intent; they are meant to make it easier for the student to decide among a number of works of apparently equal significance or relevance. Where a single work contains more than one contribution, I have adopted the policy of listing all the entries together as one item under the title of the volume.

No entries by Kierkegaard have been included in this listing; the only appropriate statement would have been, "Read all his work." The serious student will discover Kierkegaard on his own, perhaps beginning with *Either/Or.*

Nietzsche, who is also a contemporary in spirit, might best be approached through *Beyond Good and Evil*.

The bibliography is divided into four sections. The first comprises original contributions by those who might be considered founding figures or enduring influences within phenomenology or existentialism. Almost none of their work was originally in English, and thus far not much has been translated. The second section consists of writing about, or in some instances reports on, the basic works of the contributors to Section I. The third section contains contributions of somewhat lesser importance as well as writings on various related topics and those which are derivative from or based upon the major works. In the fourth section I have gathered a small group of items that will provide an introduction to the field of existential psychotherapy. This is a clinical specialty derived from phenomenological and existential conceptions and rapidly becoming an important orientation toward the treatment of emotional problems. Within each of these sections the listing is alphabetical by author and chronological when he is represented by more than one entry. The full bibliography, however, is numbered sequentially. In a special, unnumbered grouping at the end I have listed some non-English works which constitute a basic reading list for those who are competent in other languages.

For those who wish to pursue some of these topics further, a number of journals are now available. *Philosophy and Phenomenological Research* carries on the tradition of classical phenomenology established by Edmund Husserl; it is written for students and scholars on the professional level. *Philosophy Today* publishes reprints and translations of many important papers in this field. *Cross Currents* contains original contributions and is a valuable source for articles in English. Two publications have recently begun specifically in the fields of existential psychology and psychiatry: *Review of Existential Psychology and Psychiatry*, published by the American Association of Existential Psychology and Psychiatry; and *The Journal of Existential Psychiatry,* published by the American Ontoanalytic Society.

Section I

1. BINSWANGER, L. On the relationship between Husserl's phenomenology and psychological insight. *Phil. Phenomenol. Res.,* 1941-42, 2, 199-210.

   Particularly good with regard to the psychological significance of the phenomenological method.

2. BINSWANGER, L. Existential analysis and psychotherapy. In F. Fromm-Reichman & J. L. Moreno (eds.), *Progress in psychotherapy, 1956.* New York: Grune & Stratton, 1956. Pp. 144-148.

3. BINSWANGER, L. Existential analysis and psychotherapy. *Psychoanal. & Psychoanal. Rev.,* 1958, 45, 79-83.

4. BOSS, M. *Meaning and content of sexual perversions: A daseinsanalytic approach to the psychopathology of the phenomenon of love.* New York: Grune & Stratton, 1949.

   Promises a great deal, particularly in the introduction, but provides mainly a hasty application of new terms to old therapeutic issues.

5. BUBER, M. *I and thou.* New York: Scribner, 1958.

   The first English edition of this little classic appeared in 1937. It is poetic, mystic, and profound.

6. BUBER, M. *Between man and man.* Boston: Beacon Press, 1955.

   "Fills out and applies" what was stated in *I and thou.* Contains a series of lectures entitled "What is man?" in which he brilliantly discusses Hegel, Marx, Feuerbach, Nietzsche, Heidegger, Scheler, and his own "philosophical anthropology."

7. BUBER, M. The William Alanson White memorial lectures, fourth series. *Psychiat.*, 1957, 20, 95-129.

   Includes lectures on distance, on "the social a d interhuman," and on guilt.

8 BUYTENDIJK, F. J. J. *The mind of the dog.* Bost : Houghton Mifflin, 1936.

9 BUYTENDIJK, F. J. J. Experienced freedom and mor l freedom in the child's consciousness. *Educ. Theory*, 1953, 3, 1-13.

10. BUYTENDIJK, F. J. J. The function of the parts within the structure of the whole: The excitability of the nerves as a phenomenon of life. *J. Indiv. Psychol*, 1959, 15, 73-78.

    A physiological problem is seen in a new light, based on the conception of "being-together of living beings and environmental events."

11 FRANKL, V. E. *The doctor and the soul: An introduction to logotherapy.* New York: Knopf, 1955.

12. HEIDEGGER, M *Existence and being.* Chicago: Regnery, 1949.

    This is the basic presentation in English of Heidegger's ideas. It contains a 235-page introduction by Werner Brock, consisting of a biographical sketch of Heidegger, an excellent account of his fundamental work, *Sein und Zeit* (Being and Time), and an account of the four essays which comprise the remainder of the volume: On the essence of truth; What is metaphysics; and two essays on the German poet Hoelderlin. A brief preface about Heidegger, from an article by Schimanski (59), discusses the philosopher as a person.

13. HEIDEGGER, M. The way back into the ground of metaphysics. In W. A. Kaufmann (ed.), *Existential-*

ism from Dostoevsky to Sartre. New York: Meridian, 1956, Pp. 206-221.

This is an introduction, translated by Kaufmann, to the essay, "What is metaphysics?" which is included in Heidegger (12).

14. HUSSERL, E. Phenomenology. In *Encycl. Brit.* (14th ed.), 1929, 17, 699-702.

This article, translated by C. V. Salmon, is the only brief presentation of his own views which is available in English. Difficult reading, but as adequate a summary as one can get.

15. JASPERS, K. On my philosophy. In W. A. Kaufmann (ed.), *Existentialism from Dostoevsky to Sartre.* New York: Meridian, 1956. Pp. 131-158.

A good introduction to Jaspers as a person, with a lot of material on his views concerning science.

16. MARCEL, G. *The philosophy of existence.* London: Harvill, 1948.

This basic work of the leading French Catholic existentialist contains an excellent autobiographical essay.

17. MAY, R., E. ANGEL, & H. F. ELLENBERGER (eds.). *Existence: A new dimension in psychiatry and psychology.* New York: Basic Books, 1958.

This volume, dedicated to Minkowski and Binswanger, contains the first collection of significant contributions in the field. There are two essays by May and one by Ellenberger, theoretical papers by Straus and Binswanger, and translations of cases by Binswanger, Minkowski, Von Gebsattel, and Kuhn.

18. MERLEAU-PONTY, M. What is phenomenology. *Cross Currents,* 1956, 6, 59-70.

19. MINKOWSKI, E. Bergson's conceptions as applied to psycho-pathology. *J. Nerv. Ment. Dis.,* 1926, 63, 553-568.

This paper, translated by F. J. Farnell, is of value for historical as well as theoretical reasons, since Bergson's ideas provided the starting point for Minkowski's contributions to the study of time.

20. SARTRE, J. P. *The emotions: Outline of a theory*. New York: Philosophical Library, 1948.

The introduction distinguishes between phenomenology as a method and psychology as a science. The book itself may be read as an exemplification of the difference between a pure phenomenology and a phenomenological psychology.

21. SARTRE, J. P. *Existentialism*. New York: Philosophical Library, 1947.

22. SARTRE, J. P. *The psychology of imagination*. New York: Philosophical Library, 1948.

Particularly interesting for its treatment (Chap. 2) of "the image family," with regard to the problem of ambiguous stimuli.

23. SARTRE, J. P. *Anti-semite and Jew*. New York: Schocken, 1948.

This penetrating study demonstrates the possibilities in the application of a phenomenological approach to social issues.

24. SARTRE, J. P. *Existential psychoanalysis*. New York: Philosophical Library, 1953.

Contains a 37-page introduction by the translator and a number of extracts from Sartre's major work, *Being and Nothingness* (1956).

25. SCHELER, M. F. *The nature of sympathy*. London: Routledge & Kegan Paul, 1954.

Except for Sartre's writings, this treatise on love and sympathy is the only full-scale work in English on the psychology of emotion. It is a translation of his "The essence and forms of sympathy" (1931), which is Vol. I of his major work, "The intrinsic structural laws of the emotional life."

26. STRAUS, E. W. Disorders of personal time in depressive states. *South. Med. J.*, 1947, 40, 254-259.

    An excellent example of the phenomenological approach to the problems of a clinical science (see also 27 and 29).

27. STRAUS, E. W. *On obsession: A clinical and methodological study.* New York: Nerv. and Ment. Dis. Monogr., 1948 (Whole No. 73).

28. STRAUS, E. W. The upright posture. *Psychiat. Quart.*, 1952, 26, 529-561.

    In this classic paper both aspects of the phenomenological-existential orientation, a descriptive phenomenology and a philosophical anthropology, are shown.

29. STRAUS, E. W. The sigh: An introduction to a theory of expression. *Tijdschr, Phil.*, 1952, 14, 1-22.

30. STRAUS, E. W. Man, a questioning being. *Tijdschr. Phil*, 1955, 17, 3-29.

31. STRAUS, E. W. Some remarks on awakeness. *Tijdschr. Phil.*, 1956, 18, 1-20.

32. STRAUS, E. W. The Fourth International Congress of Psychotherapy, Barcelona, Spain, September 1 through 7, 1958. *Psychosom. Med.*, 1959, 21, 158-164.

    Reviews the background and proceedings of the Congress, particularly in reference to the place of existentialism in the history of science.

33. TILLICH, P. *The courage to be.* New Haven: Yale Univer. Press, 1952.

34. TILLICH, P. *Theology of culture.* New York: Oxford Univer. Press, 1959.

Section II

35. BARRETT, W. *Irrational man: A study in existential philosophy*. New York: Doubleday, 1958.
    From the point of view of style or historical background, this is the best of the recent commentaries.

36. BLACKHAM, H. J. *Six existentialist thinkers*. New York: Macmillan, 1952.

37. BLAUNER, J. Existential analysis: L. Binswanger's Daseinsanalyse. *Psychoanal. Rev.*, 1957, 44, 51-64.
    Oversimplifies many of the concepts, but it provides a good summary of Binswanger's major work.

38. BLEULER, M. Researches and changes in concepts in the study of schizophrenia. *Bull. Isaac Ray Med. Libr.*, 1955, 3, 42-45.

39. COLLINS, J. D. *The existentialists: A critical study*. Chicago: Regnery, 1952.

40. CREEGAN, R. F. Phenomenology. In P. L. Harriman (ed.), *Encyclopaedia of psychology*. New York: Philosophical Library, 1946, Pp. 512-515.

41. DESAN, W. *The tragic finale*. Cambridge: Harvard Univer. Press, 1954.
    Mildly critical essay on Sartre, with an appendix on Sartre and Freud.

42. ELLENBERGER, H. F. Current trends in European psychotherapy. *Amer. J. Psychother.*, 1953, 7, 733-753.
    Contains his own discussion of Szondi and Binswanger, plus some discussion by others.

43. FARBER, M. *The foundation of phenomenology: Edmund Husserl and the quest for a rigorous science of philosophy*. Cambridge: Harvard Univer. Press. 1943.

The first seven chapters contain a full history of Husserl's early work.

44. GRENE, M. *Dreadful freedom: A critique of existentialism.* Chicago: Univer. of Chicago Press, 1948.

Reissued in 1959, in the Phoenix paperback series of the University of Chicago Press, as *Introduction to existentialism.*

45. KAHN, E. An appraisal of existential analysis. *Psychiat. Quart.,* 1957, 31, 203-227, 417-444.

Contains a historical survey, with extensive quotations from original sources; the material selected serves mainly as a target for criticism.

46. KUHN, H. *Encounter with nothingness: A study on existentialism.* Chicago: Regnery, 1949.

This book and the essay by Natanson (56) are possibly the most authoritative of the recent commentaries on Sartre.

47. LANDSMAN, T. Four phenomenologies. *J. Indiv. Psychol.,* 1958, 14, 29-37.

Useful for the student, but necessarily very compressed.

48. LAUER, Q. Four phenomenologies. *Thought,* 1958, 33, 183-204.

A discussion of four European figures—Heidegger and Scheler in Germany, and Merleau-Ponty and Sartre in France.

49. LEDERMAN, E. K. A review of the principles of Adlerian psychology. *Int. J. Soc. Psychiat.,* 1956, 2, 172-184.

Contains some material on its relationship with existential philosophy.

50. LEFEBRE, L. B. Report on the 4th International Congress of Psychotherapy. *Amer. J. Psychother.,* 1959, 13, 111-120.

A sound summary, especially with regard to the key figures and the issue of the relation between Freud and the existential analysts.

51. LOEWENBERG, R. D. Karl Jaspers on psychotherapy. *Amer. J. Psychother.*, 1951, 5, 502-513.

52. MACQUARRIE, J. *An existentialist theology: A comparison of Heidegger and Bultmann.* New York: Macmillan, 1955.

A very lucid exposition of Heidegger's position on many issues, comparing him point by point with the Protestant theologian.

53. MUELLER-FREIENFELS, R. *The evolution of modern psychology.* New Haven: Yale Univer. Press, 1935. Pp. 310-314.

One has to read the entire book to appreciate the background of his remarks, but this section deserves particular study.

54. MURDOCH, I. *Sartre.* New Haven: Yale Univer. Press, 1953.

Since Sartre's thinking can best be understood in the light of all his writings, including the purely literary works, this fine critique is especially valuable.

55. MUUS, R. Existentialism and psychology. *Educ. Theory,* 1956, 6, 135-153.

56. NATANSON, M. *A critique of Jean Paul Sartre's ontology.* (Univer. of Nebraska Studies, New series, No. 6), Lincoln: Univer. of Nebraska Press, 1951.

A competent and sympathetic survey by a philosopher.

57. PERVIN, L. A. Existentialism, psychology, and psychotherapy. *Amer. Psychol.*, 1960, 15, 305-309.

58. POLAK, P. Frankl's *Existential Analysis. Amer. J. Psychother.*, 1949, 3, 617-622.

59. SCHIMANSKI, S. On meeting a philosopher. *Partisan Rev.*, 1948, 15, 506-511.

    A portion of this paper is printed as a preface in a book by Heidegger (12).

60. SCHMIDL, F. Sigmund Freud and Ludwig Binswanger. *Psychonal. Quart.*, 1959, 28, 40-58.

61. SILVERMAN, H. L. The philosophy and psychology of existentialism. *Psychiat. Quart. Suppl.*, 1947, 21, 10-16.

62. SONNEMAN, U. Existential analysis; An introduction to its theory and methods. *Cross Currents*, 1955, No. 3.

63 SONNEMAN, U. *Existence and therapy: An introduction to phenomenological psychology and existential analysis.* New York: Grune & Stratton, 1954.

    The soundest and most complete coverage of the subject in English, unfortunately vitiated by a barbaric prose style.

64. SPIEGELBERG, H. French existentialism: Its social philosophies. *Kenyon Rev.*, 1954, 16, 446-462.

65 STERN, A. *Sartre: His philosophy and psychoanalysis.* New York: Liberal Arts Press, 1953.

66. STRASSER, S. Phenomenological trends in European psychology. *Phil. Phenomenol. Res.*, 1956-57, 18, 18-34.

67. TIEBOUT, H. M., Jr. Freud and existentialism. *J. nerv. Ment. Dis.*, 1958, 126, 341-352.

68 TILLICH, P. Existential philosophy. *J. Hist. Ideas*, 1944, 5, 44-70.

69. VAN DEN BERG, J. H. *The phenomenological approach to psychiatry.* Springfield, Ill.: Thomas, 1955.

    Readable but quite elementary.

70. VAN DUSEN, W. The theory and practice of existential analysis. *Amer. J. Psychother.*, 1957, 11, 310-322.

    A sensible and useful overview on an introductory level.

71. VAN DUSEN, W. Adler and existence analysis. *J. Indiv. Psychol.*, 1959, 15, 100-111.

72. WAHL, J. *A short history of existentialism.* New York: Philosophical Library, 1949.

    A brief historical essay, followed by an interesting, round-robin discussion of some of Heidegger's concepts.

73. WALKER, K. F. A critique of the phenomenological theory of behavior. *Aust. J. Psychol.*, 1957, 9, 97-104.

74. WEIGERT, E. Existentialism and its relations to psychotherapy. *Psychiat.*, 1949, 12, 399-412.

    A good summary of the conceptions that Binswanger took over from Heidegger.

75. WEISSKOPF-JOELSON, E. Some comments on a Viennese school of psychiatry. *J. Abnorm. Soc. Psychol.*, 1955, 51, 701-703.

76. WEISSKOPF-JOELSON, E. Logotherapy and existential analysis. *Acta Psychotherapeut.*, 1958, 6, 193-204.

77. WILD, J. *The challenge of existentialism.* Bloomington: Indiana Univer. Press, 1955.

78. WILD, J. Is there a world of ordinary language? *Philos. Rev.*, 1958, 68, 460-476.

    A distinguished philosopher discusses some fundamental problems in a most helpful fashion.

79. WYSCHOGROD, M. *Kierkegaard and Heidegger: The ontology of existence.* New York: Humanities Press, 1954.

    Presents the two philosophers in alternate chapters.

A difficult book, written in craggy prose, but highly rewarding if one is prepared to read it.

Section III

80. ALLPORT, G. W. *Becoming: Basic considerations for a psychology of personality*. New Haven: Yale Univer. Press, 1955.

    A brief presentation and platform which is approximately within the phenomenological orientation.

81. ARENDT, H. *The human condition*. Chicago: Univer. of Chicago Press, 1958.

    A work of superb scholarship, probably the best attempt in English to apply Heidegger's teachings to meaningful social problems.

82. BECK, M. The proper object of psychology. *Phil. Phenomenol. Res.*, 1952-53, 13, 285-304.

83. BECK, S. J. Implications for ego in Tillich's ontology on anxiety. *Phil. Phenomenol. Res.*, 1956-57, 17, 451-470.

84. BINSWANGER, L. *Sigmund Freud: Reminiscences of a friendship*. New York: Grune & Stratton, 1957.

    This report of a lifelong friendship is of value for understanding the relation of Binswanger's "system" to psychoanalytic theory and practice.

85. BINSWANGER, L. Symptoms and time: A casuistic contribution. *Existent. Inqu.*, 1960, 1 (2), 14-18.

86. BLUMENFELD, W. Observations concerning the phenomenon and origin of play. *Phil. Phenomenol. Res.*, 1940-41, 1, 470-478.

87. Boss, M. Mechanistic and holistic thinking in modern medicine. *Amer. J. Psychoanal.*, 1954, 14, 48-54.

88. Boss, M. *The analysis of dreams.* New York: Philosophical Library, 1958.

An authorized and popularized statement of Heidegger's views, particularly in respect to his disagreement with the Freudians and with Binswanger.

89. Buytendijk, F. J. J. Philosophic basis of human relations. *Philos. Today,* 1958, 2, 108-112.

90. Buytendijk, F. J. J. The meaning of pain. *Philos. Today,* 1959, 3/4, 180-185.

91. Combs, A. W. Phenomenological concepts in nondirective therapy. *J. Consult. Psychol.,* 1948, 12, 197-208.

92. Combs, A. W. A phenomenological approach to adjustment theory. *J. Abnorm. Soc. Psychol.,* 1949, 44, 29-39.

93. Combs, A. W., & D. Snygg. *Individual behavior: A perceptual approach to behavior.* (Rev. ed.) New York: Harper, 1959.

This is a revision of an earlier work (1949), which first stated the position of the "American" school of phenomenology.

94. Creegan, R. F. The phenomenological analysis of personal documents. *J. Abnorm. Soc. Psychol.,* 1944, 39, 244-266.

95. Creegan, R. F. Remarks on the phenomenology of praise. *Phil. Phenomenol. Res.,* 1945-46, 6, 421-423.

96. Creegan, R. F. A phenomenological critique of psychology. *Phil. Phenomenol. Res.,* 1948-49, 9, 309-315.

97. David, H. P., & H. von Bracken (eds.). *Perspectives in personality theory.* New York: Basic Books, 1957.

The following contributions are of interest : (a) A. Wellek, The phenomenological and experimental approaches to psychology and characterology, pp.

278-299. Presents one side of an argument with Eysenck on some fundamental issues. (b) J. NUTTIN, Personality dynamics, pp. 183-195. His usual sound, quasi-phenomenological treatment. (c) D. J. VAN LENNEP, Projection and personality, pp. 259-277. Rather general in treatment, not too useful. (d) F. J. J. BUYTENDIJK, Femininity and existential psychology, pp. 197-211. Essentially a summary of his larger work on this subject.

98. DE BEAUVOIR, S. *The second sex.* New York: Knopf, 1953.

This work demonstrates the provocative treatment of a problem when the view is informed with an existentialist perspective.

99. DE LAUROT, E. L. Toward a theory of dynamic realism. *Film Culture,* 1955, 1, 2-14.

100. DE LAUROT, E. L. On critics and criteria. *Film Culture,* 1955, 1(2), 4-11.

These two essays on the art of the film are based on Sartre's thinking.

101. DELIUS, H. Descriptive interpretation. *Phil. Phenomenol. Res.,* 1953, 13, 305-323.

As essay, based on Heidegger's ideas, on the problem of phenomenological description.

102. DUNCKER, K. On pleasure, emotion, and striving. *Phil. Phenomenol. Res.,* 1940-41, 1, 391-430.

This is a chapter from his unfinished book on motivation.

103. FARBER, M. (ed.). *Philosophical essays in memory of Edmund Husserl.* Cambridge: Harvard Univer. Press, 1940.

See in particular the papers by Alfred Schuetz on phenomenology and the social sciences and by John Wild on phenomenology and "psychologism."

104. FARBER, M. L. Time perspective and feeling-tone: A study in the perception of the days. *J. Psychol.*, 1953, 35, 253-257.

105. FRANKL, V. E. Logos and existence in psychotherapy. *Amer. J. Psychother.*, 1953, 7, 8-15.

106. FRANKL, V. E. *From death-camp to existentialism: A psychiatrist's path to a new therapy.* Boston: Beacon Press, 1959.
Contains a very moving account of his experiences in a concentration camp and the effect this had on his thinking.

107. FROMM, E. *Escape from freedom.* New York: Rinehart, 1941.

108. FROMM, E. *Man for himself.* New York: Rinehart, 1947.

109. GAFFRON, M. Some new dimensions in the phenomenal analysis of visual experience. *J. Pers.*, 1956, 24, 285-307.
A good instance of the phenomenological method as applied to a specific experimental problem (see also 161).

110. GOLDSTEIN, K. The smiling of the infant and the problem of understanding the other. *J. Psychol.*, 1957.

111. GURWITSCH, A. The phenomenological and the psychological approach to consciousness. *Phil. Phenomenol. Res.*, 1954-55, 15, 303-319.
An excellent comparison with regard to some basic problems.

112. HARTGENBUSCH, H. G. Gestalt psychology in sport. *Psyche*, 1927, 27, 41-52.

113. HEIDER, F. Social perception and phenomenal causality. *Psychol. Rev.*, 1944, 51, 358-374.
This has been reprinted as Chap. 1, pp. 1-21, of

R. Tagiuri & L. Petrullo (eds.), *Person perception and interpersonal behavior* (Stanford, Calif.: Stanford Univer. Press, 1958).

114. JONAS, H. The nobility of sight. *Phil. Phenomenol. Res.*, 1953-54, 14, 507-519.

This is one of the rare pieces in English on the phenomenology of sensory experience, although the topic is of central importance in this orientation.

115. KATZ, D. *The world of colour*. London: Kegan Paul, Trench, Trubner, 1935.

This is a pre-eminent classic in the field; of particular interest is the large number of experiments reported in this work.

116. KOYRE, A. Influence of philosophical trends on the formulation of scientific theories. *Sci. Mon.*, 1955, 80, 107-111.

117. KUENZLI, A. (ed.). *The phenomenological problem*. New York: Harper, 1959.

One of the best introductory sources for papers by some of the leading American figures.

118. LANGEVELD, M. J. (ed.). *Rencontre-Encounter-Begegnung.* (Contributions to one human psychology, dedicated to Professor F. J. J. Buytendijk.) Utrecht: Spectrum, 1958.

This memorial volume to one of the foremost figures in European phenomenology contains the following relevant papers in English: (a) F. J. TH. RUTTEN, On social and collective psychology, pp. 438-455. A series of observations, raising some very provocative questions. (b) H. C. J. DUIJKER, The initial stages of social contact, pp. 129-139. A "sociopsychological" study. (c) L. VAN DER HORST, Psychopathology and multisignificant symbolism, pp. 221-228. (d) D. J. VAN LENNEP, The forgotten time in applied psychology, pp. 256-259. Demonstrates the "practical" applications of phenomenological conceptions of time.

119. LEIBRECHT, W. *Religion and culture: Essays in honor of Paul Tillich.* New York: Harper, 1959.
    Uneven, as are most such *Festschriften,* but of some interest are the essays by Lowith, Takeuchi, Jaspers, and Marcel.

120. LYONS, J. The psychology of angels. *Forum,* 1958, 2, 28-30.

121. LYONS, J. Magic, fate, and delusion. *Forum,* 1959, 3, 18-21.

122. LYONS, J. An interview with a mute catatonic. *J. Abnorm. Soc. Psychol.,* 1960, 60, 271-277.

123. MACLEOD, R. B. The phenomenological approach to social psychology. *Psychol. Rev.,* 1947, 54, 193-210.
    The first and only paper on classical phenomenology in an American journal of psychology. Very little of what is proposed here has been picked up, but it may profitably be restudied. Reprinted as pp. 33-53 in the Tagiuri-Petrullo book (113).

124. MACLEOD, R. B. The place of phenomenological analysis in social psychological theory. In J. H. Rohrer & M. Sherif (eds.), *Social psychology at the crossroads.* New York: Harper, 1951. Pp. 215-241.

125. MAY, R. *The meaning of anxiety.* New York: Ronald, 1950.

126. MAY, R. *Man's search for himself.* New York: Norton, 1953.

127. MAY, R. The nature of creativity. In Anderson (ed.), *Creativity and its cultivation.* New York: Harper, 1959.

128. McGILL, V. J. The bearing of phenomenology on psychology. *Phil. Phenomenol. Res.*, 1947, 7, 357-368.
     Very much to the point with regard to methodology.

129. McGILL, V. J. Some issues in current psychological literature. *Phil. Phenomenol. Res.*, 1956-57, 17, 89-104.

130. NIEBUHR, R. Limitations of the scientific method: An answer to Pierre Auger. *Bull. Atom. Sci.*, 1955, 11, 87.

131. NUTTIN, J. Consciousness, behavior, and personality *Psychol. Rev.*, 1955, 62, 349-355.
     This paper, based rather remotely on Husserl, makes a good start for study of these issues.

132. PERCY, W. The loss of the creature. *Forum*, 1958, 2, 6-14.

133. REYMERT, M. L. (ed.). *Feelings and emotions: The Mooseheart Symposium.* New York: McGraw-Hill, 1950.
     This volume contains two papers of interest: (a) . J. BUYTENDIJK, The phenomenological approach to the problem of feelings and emotions. A difficult piece, requiring some background, but worth studying carefully. (b) J. NUTTIN, Intimacy and shame in the dynamic structure of the personality. Somewhat marginal to a phenomenological orientation, but intelligent and unobjectionable.

1 4. ROGERS, C. R. Person or science? A philosophica question. *Amer. Psychol.*, 1955, 10, 267-278.

1ɔ5. SARTRE, J. P. *No exit and 3 other plays.* New York: Vintage, 1955.
     The flies may be read as an essay on memory and

guilt, and *No exit* as a statement on the psychology of interpersonal relations.

136. SARTRE, J. P. *Literary essays*. New York: Philosophical Library, 1957.
Contains brilliant essays on freedom, the absurd, the philosophy of Aristotle, the fantastic, illusion, time, and aesthetic distance.

137. SCHACHTEL, E. The dynamic perception and the symbolism of form: With special reference to the Rorschach test. *Psychiat.*, 1941, 4, 79-96.

138. SCHACHTEL, E. On color and affect: Contribution to an understanding of Rorschach's test: II. *Psychiat.*, 1943, 6, 393-409.

139. SCHACHTEL, E. The development of focal attention and the emergence of reality. *Psychiat.*, 1954, 17, 309-324.

140. SCHACHTEL, E. *Metamorphosis: On the development of affect, perception, attention, and memory*. New York: Basic Books, 1959.
An important work, by a man who has been influenced by both the psychoanalytic and phenomenological movements.

141. SCHUETZ, A. Common-sense and scientific interpretation of human action. *Phil. Phenomenol. Res.*, 1953-54, 14, 1-37.

142. SMEDSLUND, J. The epistemological foundations of behaviorism: A critique. *Acta Psychol.*, 1955, 11, 412-431.

143. SMITH, M. B. The phenomenological approach in personality theory: Some critical remarks. *J. Abnorm. Soc. Psychol.*, 1950, 45, 516-522.
See also Snygg and Combs (145).

144. SNYGG, D. The need for a phenomenological system of psychology. *Psychol. Rev.*, 1941, 48, 404-424.

   Discusses in detail some problems of learning theory and asks for a "Gestalt psychology along phenomenological lines."

145. SNYGG, D. & A. W. COMBS. The phenomenological approach and the problem of "unconscious" behavior: A reply to Dr. Smith. *J. Abnor. Soc. Psychol.*, 1950, 45, 523-528.

   See also Smith (143).

146. SONNEMAN, U. The specialist as a psychological problem. *Soc. Res.*, 1951, 18, 9-31.

   This is written in a surprisingly clear style.

147. SONNEMAN, U. The human sciences and spontaneity: Outline of a revolution. *Amer. J. Psychoanal.*, 1958, 18, 138-148.

   One of the best phenomenological accounts of what Straus has called "the human world," the subject matter for a psychological science.

148. STERN, A. Existential psychoanalysis and individual psychology. *J. Indiv. Psychol.*, 1958, 14, 38-50.

149. STRAUS, E. W. Rheoscopic studies of expression: Methodology of approach. *Amer. J. Psychiat.*, 1951, 108, 439-443.

   A method and technique based on phenomenological considerations is applied to the problem of the study of expression.

150. STRAUS, E. W., & R. M. GRIFFITH. Pseudo-reversibility of catatonic stupor. *Amer. J. Psychiat.*, 1955, 111, 680-685.

151. STRAUS, E. W. On the form and structure of Man's inner freedom. *Ky. Law J.*, 1956-57, 45, 255-269.

152. TILLICH, P. Anxiety, religion, and medicine. *Pastoral Psychol.*, 1952, 3, 11-17.

153. TILLICH, P. Being and love. *Pastoral Psychol.*, 1954, 5(43), 43-48.

154. TILLICH, P. Psychoanalysis, existentialism and theology. *Pastoral Psychol.*, 1958, 9, 9-17.

155. TOLSMA, F. J. Some considerations on the phenomenon of aggression. *J. Ment. Sci.*, 1953, 99, 473-482.

156. VAN DEN BERG, J. H. The human body and the significance of human movement. *Phil. Phenomenol. Res.*, 1952-53, 13, 159-183.

157. VAN DEN BERG, J. H. The handshake. *Philos. Today*, 1959, 3/4, 28-34.

158. VAN DER HORST, L. Mental health and religion. *Pastoral Psychol.*, 1955, 6, 15-21.

159. VAN DER HORST, L. The philosophical and psychiatric basis of psychosomatic medicine. *Acta Psychother. Psychosom. Orthopaedagog.*, 1957, 5, 1-9.

160. VAN KAAM, A. Assumptions in psychology. *J. Indiv. Psychol.*, 1958, 14, 22-28.

161. VAN KAAM, A. L. Phenomenal analysis: Exemplified by a study of the experience of "really feeling understood." *J. Indiv. Psychol.*, 1959, 15, 66-72.

162. VON HORNBOSTEL, E. M. The unity of the senses. *Psyche*, 1927, 7, 83-89.
   This fascinating essay is reprinted in W. D. Ellis (ed.), *A source book of Gestalt psychology* (New York: Humanities Press, 1950).

163. VON UEXKUELL, J. *Theoretical biology.* London: Kegan Paul, Trench, Trubner, 1926.
   This is one of the earliest works in a related science to be influenced by Husserl's ideas.

164. WOLFF, W. *Values and personality: An existential psychology of crisis.* New York: Grune & Stratton, 1950.

One of the very early books in this field, and something of a potboiler.

Section IV

165. COLM, H. Healing as participation: Comments based on Paul Tillich's existential philosophy. *Psychiat.*, 1953, 16, 99-111.

166. ELLENBERGER, H. F. Phenomenology and existential analysis. *Canad. Psychiat. Assoc. J.*, 1957, 2, 137-146.

167. FRANKL, V. E. On logotherapy and existential analysis. *Amer. J. Psychoanal.*, 1958, 18, 28-37.

168. HORA, T. Existential communication and psychotherapy. *Psychoanal.*, 1957, 5, 38-45.

169. HORA, T. Existential group psychotherapy. *Amer. J. Psychotherap.*, 1959, 13, 83-92.

170. HORA, T. Psychotherapy, existence, and religion. *Psychoanal. & Psychoanal. Rev.*, 1959, 46, 91-98.

171. MAY, R. (ed.). *Symbols in Religion and Literature.* New York: George Braziller, 1960.

172. MULLAN, H., & I. SANGIULIANO. Interpretation as existence in analysis. *Psychoanal. & Psychoanal. Rev.*, 1958, 45, 52-73.

173. ROGERS, C. R. To be is to do. Review of *Existence. Contemporary Psychol.*, 1959, July, vol. IV, No. 7. (See 17).

174. TILLICH, P. Existentialism and psychotherapy. *Existent. Inqu.*, 1960, 1(3).

175. VAN DUSEN, W. Zen and Western psychotherapy. *Psychologia*, 1958, 1, 229-230.

176. VAN KAAM, A. The impact of existential phenomenology on the psychological literature of Western Europe. *Review of Existential Psychology and Psychiatry*, 1 (1), 1961, 62-91.

177. WENKART, A. The creative power of relatedness. *Amer. J. Psychoanal.*, 1956, 14, 125-132.

NOTE: See also the essay, "Contributions of existential psychotherapy," by Rollo May in *Existence* (17).

Basic, Untranslated Works

BINSWANGER, L. *Grundformen und Erkenntnis menschlichen Daseins.* [Fundamental forms and understanding of human existence.] Zurich: Verlag Max Niehaus, 1953.
　　The basic presentation of his application of Heidegger.

BINSWANGER, L. *Schizophrenie.* [Schizophrenia.] Pfullingen: Neske, 1957.
　　Contains a brief introduction plus the full text of his five famous cases: Ellen West, Ilse [both translated in 17], Jürg Zünd, Lola Voss, and Suzanne Urban.

HEIDEGGER, M. *Sein und Zeit.* [Being and time.] Halle: Max Niemeyer, 1927.

JASPERS, K. *Allgemeine Psychopathologie.* [General psychopathology.] (5th ed.) Berlin: Springer, 1946.

JASPERS, K. *Psychologie der Weltanschauungen.* [Psychology of world-views.] (4th ed.) Berlin: Springer, 1954.

MERLEAU-PONTY, M. *Phénoménologie de la perception.* [Phenomenology of perception.] (4th ed.) Paris: Gallimard, 1945.

MINKOWSKI, E. *Le temps vécu: Etudes phénoménologiques et psychopathologiques.* [Time as experienced: Phenomenological and psychopathological studies.] Paris: J. L. L. D'Artrey, 1933.

STRAUS, E. W. *Vom Sinn der Sinne*. [On the meaning of the senses.] (2d ed.) Berlin: Springer, 1956.

NOTE: Although very little of Buytendijk's work has appeared in English, his important works on women, pain, play, etc., have been translated into many languages. They are available in Dutch, German, French, Italian, and Spanish. The reader with competence in any of these languages may consult the complete bibliography which is printed as an appendix to the volume edited by Langeveld (118).